Serkeftin:
A Narrative of the
Rojava Revolution

Serkeftin:
A Narrative of the
Rojava Revolution

Marcel Cartier

Winchester, UK
Washington, USA

First published by Zero Books, 2019
Zero Books is an imprint of John Hunt Publishing Ltd., No. 3 East St., Alresford,
Hampshire SO24 9EE, UK
office1@jhpbooks.net
www.johnhuntpublishing.com
www.zero-books.net

For distributor details and how to order please visit the 'Ordering' section on our website.

Text copyright: Marcel Cartier 2018

ISBN: 978 1 78904 012 8
978 1 78904 013 5 (ebook)
Library of Congress Control Number: 2018930208

A CIP catalogue record for this book is available from the British Library.

Design: Stuart Davies

Printed and bound by CPI Group (UK) Ltd, Croydon, CR0 4YY, UK

We operate a distinctive and ethical publishing philosophy in
all areas of our business, from our global network of authors to
production and worldwide distribution.

Contents

In the midst of death, I am very close to life.
Mehmet Aksoy (Firaz Dag)
1985 – eternal

Introduction

In Mehmet's Footsteps

This book wasn't supposed to happen this way. In fact, if it wasn't for the sheer motivating force of one profoundly influential human being, this book wouldn't have happened at all. It was he who was supposed to pen the first words in this volume; to set the tone for the chapters to come, to paint the backdrop of the centuries-long struggle for Kurdish freedom, to give as only he could the most comprehensive yet simple account of what the Rojava Revolution is all about. It was this often painstaking approach of his in explaining this movement that made Mehmet Aksoy such a tour-de-force in the struggle for the liberation of his people.

When I first encountered Mehmet in September of 2014, it was at an event that we were both speaking at in London which was organized by the Tricontinental Anti-Imperialist Platform. This was an initiative that I was a part of that aimed to link international struggles in a spirit of mutual respect and understanding. While my talk dealt with the question of political prisoner turned modern day escaped slave Assata Shakur, Memo (Mehmet) was there to explain the process in northern Syria that by that time had been in motion for just over 2 years. As the Syrian state had been bogged down in conflict with a number of mostly reactionary insurgent groups in other parts of the country starting in 2011, it had ceded de-facto autonomy to the Kurdish forces of the People's and Women Protection Units (YPG and YPJ) in 2012 in much of the north of the country. At the time Mehmet gave his presentation, it was all the more significant as the forces of Daesh – sometimes known as the Islamic State of Iraq and the Levant (ISIL, or ISIS) – were on the move in Kobane, attempting to take the predominately Kurdish city on the Syria-

Turkey border. What was unfolding was a battle that would soon draw comparisons to Stalingrad for its degree of heroism and human sacrifice, and ultimately for being a turning point in the war.

As Mehmet was introduced and took to the podium, I grabbed my camera and began filming his talk. On this day, I was juggling multiple tasks as an organizer, speaker and filmmaker. There were about a dozen speeches that were made over the course of roughly 3 hours. Yet, with all due respect to anyone else who may have spoken on that particular occasion – and I'm sure there were a number of great contributions – it's only Mehmet's words that I actually remember vividly. There are a few reasons for this.

On the one hand, at that time I was extremely sceptical about the so-called 'Rojava Revolution'. I had the tendency to view the war in Syria as nothing more than a proxy conflict between the United States, western and Gulf states that seemed to be infringing on Syrian sovereignty, on the one hand; and the Russian, Iranian and the Syrian state forces that looked to defend it. This meant that the notion that there was any possible 'third way' that broke this dichotomy was something I was very dismissive of. I viewed the idea that Kurds who comprised maybe only 10 to 15 per cent of Syria's population were somehow the vanguard of a revolution within a counter-revolution as ludicrous. I didn't understand the dynamics of Syrian society, even though I was a self-professed revolutionary, and even though I read the media that conformed to my worldview on a daily basis, helping to feed my biases and what I had already deemed to be true. I was a Marxist, but increasingly rigid and dogmatic in my approach to what was a fluid and contradictory situation. This was one reason that Mehmet's speech had such a profound impact on me. It began to stir something inside of me – a feeling that perhaps I didn't have all the pieces to the puzzle when it came to understanding the Syrian war, despite me thinking I had already fitted them all neatly together long before.

The other reason that Mehmet's contribution was so dynamic was his profoundly revolutionary character. He spoke with deep passion, clarity and in a way that showed he cared about reaching the audience. There was conviction, but no arrogance. There was also a very evident spirit of internationalism. He personally struck a chord in me in a huge way when he talked about Black Panther George Jackson's book *Blood In My Eye* being one of the formative texts in his political education and development. This surprised me, not only because I had expected that Mehmet would only talk about Kurdistan, but also because that book was an extremely important volume in my studies, one that I had read with huge enthusiasm when I was 17. Memo's ability to link the Kurdish struggle with the black liberation movement in the United States was impressive. It also showed me that there was no way that the process he supported in northern Syria was some kind of pseudo-revolutionary puppet movement that was objectively tied to Washington and the Pentagon.

Over the months to come, the spark that Mehmet had lit began to mature into something much greater. To be sure, he had no idea that he had this kind of impact on the charting of my political future merely by deciding to accept the invitation to speak at a relatively small event in London attended by maybe 100 people. I'm sure I'm not the only person who had been so moved by his words that it has shaken their convictions, or at least somewhat challenged their preconceptions.

As the battle for Kobane unfolded and the YPG and YPJ ultimately declared victory over the forces of fascism, my interest in the Kurdish Freedom Movement only grew. I was already making plans to eventually make it to northern Syria. The question was what role I should play. Should I travel there as an internationalist fighter? As a journalist? As a solidarity activist? I decided that I would go in whatever capacity I could be most useful. As another Black Panther, Fred Hampton, once put it – we learn best through observation and participation.

It would take me roughly another 2 years until I was able to at last make it to Rojava. The opportunity came in the form of an internationalist youth delegation from Europe. I would be among only three journalists on the trip, afforded a very unique and rare opportunity to visit the civil structures that had been set up over nearly 5 years of the revolution. This trip would initially take me to northern Iraq, then overland to northern Syria. Once there, I would spend a little over a month with unparalleled access to the organizations behind the fighters and the frontlines. I would get a sense of the kind of system and new society that those fighting and dying in the YPG and YPJ were shedding their blood for.

I had no idea what my experiences in Rojava would translate into. However, when I returned to Europe, I was so moved and motivated by what I had seen that I simply began writing, without anything resembling an end goal. I had returned with roughly 80 pages of notes that I knew contained information the world needed to acquire and understand. Within weeks, I had crafted five or six articles detailing the inner-workings of many of the structures I had been given access to.

Yet, my words weren't intended to be an academic study of the revolution. There were already enough books that did an adequate job of this, in my view. Instead, I thought it more suitable to write pieces that were full of emotion and my subjective feelings – how Rojava stirred and reignited my revolutionary fire, how it challenged my dogmatism, how it unearthed the potential for a new society and world in the midst of the most tragic and brutal war of the twenty-first century.

I knew that Mehmet was the brain behind the website *Kurdish Question* which had long been viewed as a definitive source for any news and analysis related to the struggle of the Kurdish nation. I decided to send him my first article on my experiences in Kobane, not knowing if he would accept it for publication or if it really did anything to further the conversation on the war and possibilities for a different kind of society once it was over. Within days, the article went up on the website and was also quickly posted by *TeleSUR English*. My follow up piece comparing the Kurdish movement in Syria to the parties in power in Iraqi Kurdistan was published less than a week later.

At this point, I still hadn't received any feedback from Mehmet himself, though it seemed as if he was at least enthusiastic enough about my writing to publish two articles within mere days. Finally, I received a personal note from him on 21 April. It was the first time that we had properly spoken in perhaps 2 years.

Dear Marcel,

I hope you're well.

I just wanted to thank you once again for your contributions.

They are absolutely fantastic and important additions to the discussion of what is happening in Rojava.

Both of your articles have received upwards of 3000 hits so far.

I look forward to others and am always available for anything you may need.

This was hugely motivating. Mehmet's stamp of approval gave me the inspiration to continue churning out articles at a pace that caught me off guard. I was writing with true zeal and major conviction. I was confident, bold and defiant of those who dared to criticize my perspective. However, I also aimed to adopt something that Memo himself evidently possessed – being able to argue one's point with an understanding of an adversarial perspective.

As *Kurdish Question* became the go-to publisher for all of my stories and recollections related to Rojava, Memo and I soon began discussions about turning what so far seemed like stand-alone articles into chapters that would form a full-length publication. I was perhaps more sceptical than he was about my ability to do this, or at least if it was truly necessary. After all, I didn't want to appear presumptuous that a westerner who had spent only 1 month in Rojava could be able to write with any degree of authority on such a complex and contradictory social revolution. Still, Memo was encouraging, arguing that it would help to foster an understanding of the Kurdish Freedom Movement, and in this sense would be a valuable contribution.

Memo soon began to take a longer period of time to respond to my emails and to upload any content onto the website. I had a sense that perhaps he had followed through on something that I knew he had been moving towards doing for quite some time. My intuition told me that there was a very good reason for his lapse in communication. Sure enough, when he finally surfaced on 24 June, he confirmed my thoughts.

Dear Marcel,

I hope I find you well. I apologise for the late response and publication. I was in transit travelling to Rojava. I'm here now and witnessing what you have written about with my own eyes and heart.

As he settled into once again being in not only his ancestral homeland but the epicentre of the world's most profound revolutionary and anti-fascist struggle, Mehmet began to turn out the most brilliant contributions for the YPG Press Office. The fact that he was willing to exchange a relatively comfortable life in Britain for the dangers of being on the frontlines only increased my already massive amount of respect for him. I decided at this point that I would have to go ahead with the book. Given his level of access to every part of Rojavan society, it only made sense to me that in addition to Mehmet serving as editor for the project, he would also be by far the best person to write the introduction. Yet, I wasn't sure if he would actually be able to find the time given his level of commitment to on-the-ground reporting, as well as the overwhelming physical and emotional toll that war can take on someone. However, in his very characteristic and humble manner, he agreed to take on the project. I received this beautiful message from him on 12 July.

Dear Marcel,

Apologies for the late reply. I hope you're very well.

When I read your email a feeling of emotion so strong came over me that I couldn't respond immediately. That was about 5 days ago. I have been thinking about what to say and if I can do a good enough job in writing an introduction that would be worthy of your work.

I am very honoured that you would even think of and ask me. I have finally decided that with your help I could write something that could do justice to your journey through Rojava and the ideas, emotions and insights it has spawned in your mind.

Could you give me more information about how this will work. What are the deadlines and how should we proceed.

Best,

Memet

Ten days later, I received another message from him after a brief lapse in communication.

Dear Marcel,

Once again, apologies for the late reply. I'm now in Raqqa and the internet here is terrible.

I am very happy you have decided to turn your work into a book, making it a more lasting piece of work. And yes it will be a great service to the revolution and its global impact. Every new book or piece of work re-energises and keeps the revolution in the public's mind and domain.

Please keep me updated on how your work develops and once I have a chance I will read all of your work again and begin setting out how I will approach the introduction. I hope I can do it justice and match your beautiful standards.

Serkeftin heval!

M

This would be the last exchange of emails that we shared; our line of communication from here on out became via Instagram. He had set up a new account, 'firazdag', on which he was posting the most jaw-dropping photos from the frontlines. I remember questioning what appeared at first glance to be a rather strange account name, although later I realized that it was a reflection of his nom-de-guerre that he adopted in Rojava: Firaz Dag.

As summer turned to autumn, it dawned on me that my writing had come to a standstill. I began to once again question whether the book project made any sense. My biggest worry was that its contents would already be outdated, or that my perspective alone was inadequate. This was amplified by Mehmet's presence in Syria. If anyone could tell the story of the freedom struggle of not only the Kurdish people but the other ethnic groups making up the Democratic Federation of Northern Syria, surely it was Memo who was living and breathing every second of the revolution at this present moment. I made sure that I let him know at every opportunity just how influential his work was for those living outside of the Middle East. On 19 September, I would receive his final message.

'Heval Marcel, thank you for your warming message and kindness. I hope I am being of some good. How are you? What is your situation and the latest with the book?'

Exactly one week later, Mehmet's spirit became eternal. He transitioned into the glorious domain of the shehids, or martyrs. I will never forget the moment that I received the news of his passing, in which my world seemed to turn upside down, in which it seemed like the forces of darkness and evil had scored a temporary victory. To take such a beautiful and compassionate soul from this earth was a great crime, not simply a tragedy. I struggled to find an explanation for such a calamity and heinous outcome. Could I use words to do so? I tried, in an open letter for my comrade and friend.

Dear Mehmet,

Words don't quite seem enough to honour your memory, your vision, your sacrifice. Words can't provide a semblance of justice at capturing your tremendous energy, your strength, your compassion; to embrace your love for humanity. At a time like this, words seem feeble, seem rigid, seem even cold though they're written with the warmest sentiments and with the best of intentions. Words just don't suffice.

Maybe you were the one who best understood this. You laboured in every way possible, and while it's true that part of that was the written word, it wasn't enough for you to simply sit on the side lines. In that sense, you wrote but you weren't at all just a writer.

You gave speeches that inspired – even ones that left shivers running down the spine of those in attendance. You informed the world through the interviews that you gave in flashy television studios about the agonising plight of the Kurdish people. Yet, the last thing you were was a man of talk.

You used a camera when necessary to attempt to capture the truth, the oppression, the pain, the anguish, the joy, the struggle – but no, you weren't simply just a filmmaker.

It would be insulting to refer to you than less than you were: a revolutionary.

In my mind, this is who you were even before you embarked on your trip to Syria several months ago. It came across so crystal clear in the way that you carried yourself. It was evident in your seriousness, your attention to detail, your genuine spirit. When you asked a question about someone, it wasn't a formality. You cared. You wanted to really know the answer. This was a rare quality, to be sure. Your seriousness was offset by an almost childish joy and simplicity, a smile undoubtedly as wide and bright as the future you had the foresight to know you were a humble part of building.

You saw the future in Rojava, and it was obvious that you finally found yourself at home for the first time in your life; not only in the sense that you were once again in your ancestral motherland. You found your way to the motherland of human potential and liberation in our century. The limitations that capitalist modernity impose on all of our souls was swiftly shaken off the moment you arrived. You were finally free. Well, within of course the constrictions of having fascist forces to fight off, to decimate, to relegate to the dustbin of human history. Still, you were certain of this eventuality, so you maintained a radiant glow anyone would be envious of.

You looked at your proudest when you donned your YPG fatigues for the first time. This wasn't an arrogant or smug kind of pride, but more akin to a realisation on your end that you were slipping into the uniform that matched your internal convictions, ethics and moral code. This was the visual manifestation of the fact that you were completely committed to a cause greater than yourself, a cause that was associated with a firm rejection of individualism and embrace of hevalti, or comradeship.

Your loss makes our world feel a little less colourful, a little less beautiful, a little less caring. Maybe, though, that's just our perspective here in the western metropoles. Though your physical being may no longer be, I'm certain that the way you have touched every soul you encountered in Rojava means that life there is ever more radiant and ever more full.

The Kurdish Freedom Movement views only those who have given the ultimate sacrifice of their lives as the truest of revolutionaries. I've already stated my humble opinion that contradicts this. I knew you were as revolutionary in life as you are now as a shehid, as a symbol of hope and an example to attempt to emulate.

You have enormous shoes to fill, Heval Mehmet. May this

world give us all the collective strength to live up to the task of filling them together.

Shedid Namirin!

Mehmet became eternal on 26 September 2017. His body was returned to London in late October, and he was given the most militant and beautiful farewell at Highgate Cemetery on 10 November.

In the days that followed, I was finally able to gather the strength and energy that he had left me in order to complete the process of finishing this book. It's not an exaggeration to say that without him, this collection wouldn't have materialized. Even more importantly, without his very astute way of being able to convince people of his arguments, I would have never become a supporter of the Kurdish Freedom Movement and the Rojava Revolution. This is the impact that Memo had on myself and so many others. Mehmet said that he wanted to do justice in his introduction to my 'high standards'. However, it's my sincere hope that this book lives up to a much higher standard that is synonymous with his life and legacy. He has set the bar eternally higher. From this point forward, everything I do needs to be to further the work of my comrade, friend and brother Mehmet Aksoy.

Chapter 1

Feeling the Spirit of Revolution

Just over 3 years ago, I returned to the hustle and bustle of capitalist modernity in London after spending a week in what the mainstream press has often coined 'the most insane place on the planet' – North Korea. I joked with a close friend of mine about how the first thing I should do with all the photos I took out there was to run them through a filter to make them all black and white. After all, the perception in western society of socialist countries in general – not to mention this 'hermit kingdom' – is that they are backward, dreary places. Therefore, why not take it upon myself to give the people just what they expected? In some ways, that would make for a more fascinating story than the one that I actually uncovered, which was of a quite 'normal' society, albeit a much more communal one (this doesn't mean that there aren't profound contradictions in North Korean society, of course). In this sense, it was a lively place – and certainly anything but dull or grey.

Still, I have to confess that there was a certain feeling missing within me from my experience there that I had hoped I would have found in a socialist society. It was the same hope that I carried with me when I travelled to places like Cuba – with its half a century of transformation that raised it up from a neo-colony of the US to a dignified country – or to Venezuela, which has been experiencing a rapid shift from neo-liberalism to people-centred governance. Yes, I have been in search of something more than just having my i's dotted and my t's crossed (which for many western radicals is unfortunately often just that the classics of Marx and Lenin are somehow being adhered to). I was also after a feeling, a spirit, the life and soul of revolution. This had always remained elusive.

Sensing the Collective Spirit

I do understand that here I am – a self-proclaimed leftist radical, a materialist – speaking in terms of *feelings*. Yet, it was exactly this concept that I found not only resonated with other internationalists in Rojava, but with revolutionaries there, in general. After having spent my first week in northern Syria in Qamishlo, one of the hevals (comrades) whom I had been with since day one turned to me and asked if I had any reflections on my first several days. I talked of the impressive structures I had seen set up so far, from the communes to the cooperatives, as well as the process of political and ideological education that I was also a part of. I was impressed with the fact that from the very beginning, I hadn't been treated as a visitor or an outsider, despite the fact that my primary work there was journalistic in nature. From the moment I arrived, I was told, 'Welcome to our revolution. This is also your revolution now.' I was made to feel that I was an integral part of this, even if I struggled linguistically with just a few words of Kurmanji. There was something else, though; something that I couldn't quite explain – but when trying my best to do so anyway, this heval simply looked at me and laughed. 'I know what you mean. The comrades here will talk a lot about this with you in the time ahead. We all say the same thing – that this revolution has a certain feeling to it that you just can't explain. It has a spirit.'

I apologize to my die-hard materialists who are probably full of disappointment at the very thought of such metaphysical conclusions! However, the reality is that for the first time in my political life, I found a struggle that resonated with me on more than just a 'checking the box' level. I *felt* it profoundly. As much as I can talk about the actual societal transformation that is ongoing in the Cizire and Kobane cantons (I wasn't fortunate enough to be able to witness Afrin), there will always be a part of my experience in these magnificent places that I won't quite be able to put into words. It's something that you have to be a part of, something that draws people together and brings out the very best qualities of what it means to be human. No, this isn't meant to romanticize or fetishize the revolution that's now in its sixth year. There are certainly no lack of problems, of contradictions and of possibilities and dangers that could mean that this process could be rolled back, curtailed or even defeated. Such is the fluid nature of war, of struggle and of life.

Restoring Hope and Revolutionary Optimism

If I was to explain what my overall thoughts were about having spent a limited amount of time in Rojava, it's that it re-instilled a sense of hope into me that I have to confess on some level I had lost. When I first embraced radical left-wing political ideas a decade and a half ago in my late teens, it was as if a light had been switched on. If reading *The Communist Manifesto* was something like the flicker of the lightbulb manifesting, Lenin's *The State and Revolution* was that light beginning to shine exceptionally brightly. However, over the many years of political practice and my coming of age in an uber-capitalist society since then (in which Marxism was still going through a recovery period since the overthrow of 'actually existing socialism' in the 1989-91 era), staying the course with consistent revolutionary optimism and faith became no easy task. Some do it quite well, and many do it exceptionally better than I do or have done. Yet, there are also many who after a period of intense political struggle in their younger years in the western metropoles, become reclusive and retire into private life and the drudgery of the 9 to 5 grind. Personal responsibilities become primary responsibilities, and revolution becomes something more for bedtime reading and the occasional demonstration. I didn't want that to be me – I *urgently* didn't want that!

On some level though, I have to admit that the thought of revolution in my lifetime – even with the excitement of the seeming revival of socialist ideas in the US and Europe – still seemed quite distant. Perhaps the point was that we have been so long accustomed to losing – or at least to not really gaining – that I couldn't dare to *really* imagine the prospect of the kind of radical experiment taking place that I always dreamt could sweep the streets of New York or the neighbourhoods of Berlin. I did eventually find it, however – in the midst of a war in the Middle East, 26 years after the supposed 'end of history' and the 'final victory' of capitalism.

The Che Guevara of the United States?

There was a high level of interest in an American internationalist coming to Rojava from the US. Everywhere I went, there was a keen curiosity in the question of how to characterize where the US is heading under the Trump administration, and when – or if – a revolution is possible in the world's most powerful country. What I realized quite early on is that my politically correct answers about subjective conditions not being so favourable were never enough to please my Kurdish comrades (I would say 'hosts', but as I have already alluded to the mere idea that I was there as someone truly foreign went out of the window on day one).

For instance, one of the most powerful memories I have of my entire experience in Rojava is of an occasion I had to meet with a number of YPG commanders in Derik (in Arabic known officially as al-Malikiyah). There was one comrade in particular whose facial expression never showed the slightest hint of what he was actually thinking. I would speak, attempting to answer his questions at length and in full, and then a translator would put my words into Kurmanji. I did my best to express the fact that a revolution in the US would of course take place, but perhaps it wouldn't happen in the very near future or even in my lifetime. I explained that the sentiment of anti-communism and anti-socialism was still rather strong in the US, although it was now beginning to subside and young people were more favourable to these ideas. My 5-minute explanation of the subjective conditions was met with a simple, 'Well, it seems like you don't really believe that the revolution will happen.' I was caught off guard by that answer. I tried to rescue myself from looking foolish, or like an armchair revolutionary, or dare I say something even worse! I stumbled through my response, and then ended with a paraphrase of a quote from Che Guevara's thoughts on revolution being the process of doing 'the impossible'. To my frustration, this comrade was relentless. He didn't look impressed when he hit me back with a simple, '... and you don't think you can be the Che Guevara of the US?'

Of course, comparing myself to Che is something I had never dreamt of doing, and I was a bit uneasy that his question would even put me in the same sentence as the world's most well-known internationalist of the twentieth century. Still, his point was well taken: no matter the odds stacked against you, nothing can hold back those with the willpower to actually succeed. It reminded me of the story of when Che met Fidel in Mexico City when the two planned the logistics of the Granma expedition. Fidel was said to have looked at Che during a conversation, saying, 'Do you think I'm crazy?' to which Che replied, 'Maybe a little.' Fidel was unfazed, 'Well, a little bit of craziness is good.' Of course, both of these late revolutionaries were Marxists and materialists – but they still *believed*, against all odds and against the most adverse of conditions – that a handful of revolutionaries imbued with the spirit and the feeling of radically changing society, could overcome the most arduous of situations and claim victory. That's the very definition of revolutionary faith.

Seven Funerals, Zero Words

The morning after this all too embarrassing conversation, it continued to play in my head. It's not that I was upset in any way. Truthfully, part of my decision to come to Rojava was to re-invigorate my revolutionary zeal. I just didn't fully expect it to happen so soon, so quickly, so profoundly – or even at all, frankly. That's what caught me off guard about the evening before, and about the entire experience across the region up until this point.

It soon became early afternoon in the city of Derik, and a car affixed with a loudspeaker travelled through the streets making an announcement that I couldn't understand, but that one of the hevals mentioned was about a funeral that would be taking place in a few hours for seven shehids (martyrs) who perished fighting on the Raqqa front. There was no question about whether we would or wouldn't attend – it was our revolutionary duty to be there to see these comrades off.

A few hours later, there I was, standing in the middle of a crowd of maybe 500 people on the only rainy and overcast day I had experienced in Rojava thus far (weather, as you can imagine, that was suitable for such a sombre occasion). I wished at that moment that my knowledge of the Kurdish language was at a much higher level, but despite that, I felt something profound stirring inside of me as I attended the memorial for those young men who fell fighting against the fascist threat of Daesh.

Although I wasn't in the YPG, although I had never met any of the fallen comrades, although I probably would never end up in Raqqa, although my life in the west was completely different to that of a Kurd in Syria, it wasn't hard for me to feel what was taking place in front of my very eyes. Perhaps I said a word or two to the internationalists with me over the few hours we were there. If I did, I don't recall. I was in a zone, in a trance, in another world entirely as I watched dozens of men and women shovel enough dirt to be able to place the coffins draped in red, yellow and green 6 feet deep. I thought once more about the immense sacrifice that the people here were paying in blood, a sacrifice that can't possibly go in vain.

Positivism – and Positivity

Maybe 3 days later, I was back in Qamishlo where I would spend the majority of my time while in Syria. I was receiving an educational about the history of the Kurdish Freedom Movement, and I became struck by a passage from Abdullah Ocalan from his 'Ideological Foundations of the Nation-State':

Positivism can be circumscribed as a philosophical approach that is strictly confined to the appearance of things, which it equates with reality itself. Since in positivism appearance is reality, nothing that has no appearance can be part of reality. We know from quantum physics, astronomy, some fields of biology and even the gist of thought itself that reality occurs in worlds that are beyond observable events. The truth, in the relationship between the observed and the observer, has mystified itself to the extent that it no longer fits any physical scale or definition. Positivism denies this and thus, to an extent, resembles the idol worshipping of ancient times, where the idol constitutes the image of reality.

Now this was something that I could relate to in light of how I had been feeling for the past week and a half, but even more so in the previous few days. Certainly, it would be a concept that I would have a lot of trouble explaining to many of my western comrades. In fact, I'm almost certain that no matter what I write at this point, there will always be some first world armchair 'revolutionist' who will find more than enough to critique in my assessment. So be it. What I will say is that my access to the Rojava Revolution, my participation (albeit so far for a short period), was enough to not only re-instil the most intense revolutionary vigour in me, but enough to confirm what was in my gut – that indeed revolution has to on some basic, spiritual level be *felt*.

Thus, I have to apologize for my writing. Honestly, it will

never quite be good enough. I can attempt to say any number of things to get people to look into the Rojava Revolution, but short of people actually making the journey there to not only see it for themselves, but to deeply and profoundly *feel* it, there's nothing I can really say that will ever do justice to what I now hold deep within me. It's in part a rekindling of the love for (and faith in) humanity and for the oppressed that has burned – and flickered – for a decade and a half. But it's also something more, something that I'm sure I will attempt to explain until I'm no longer alive, but which unfortunately can't be placed in mere words. It's not that I'm keeping secrets, but maybe – just maybe – Rojava *is* holding secrets, or rather keys to the future. For that reason, those with an inkling towards social justice and the prospect of a better world coming to fruition should make the journey. I can't promise anything other than that it will forever change your life.

Chapter 2

The Epic Resistance of Kobane

Driving through the beautiful countryside of northern Syria, the tranquil atmosphere doesn't reveal the slightest possibility that this is a country that is at war, or that this area was one of the frontlines of that now 6-year conflict just a short time ago. In fact, the thought that the most extreme of fascist organizations not long ago controlled this serene landscape seems impossible.

Arriving from the east into Kobane canton, a destroyed school soon jolts one into full sobriety. A memorial in front of the remains of this centre of learning pays homage to the 13 fallen comrades of the YPG and YPJ who perished here in the fight against barbarism. At the beginning of the battle for Kobane, these courageous young women and men held this school for an entire night of battle with the advancing forces of the so-called Islamic State before running out of ammunition. When they realized that all of their possibilities of fighting back had been exhausted, they made the decision they would never be captured alive. Instead, they huddled together, sang a revolutionary song over the radio to their comrades, and with their last grenades blew themselves up. This was the spirit of resistance that made possible the victory of the YPG and YPJ in the epic that began on that night.

A few days after my first impressions of Kobane, I find myself in the heart of the city with a group of internationalists. We are looking at the destruction left behind by Daesh and the fightback waged against them by the Kurdish revolutionaries. It's hard not to feel like little more than 'revolutionary tourist' under these circumstances. It's easy to feel nauseous, in part because the stench of death – real or imagined – still lingers.

The border of Turkey is just metres away, a flag representing that country that is sliding into fascism itself hovering above a newly constructed border wall. At the time of the battle between September 2014 and January 2015, that wall didn't exist, meaning that forces of both Daesh and the Turkish state could enter and exit Kobane as they saw fit. The stories of Turkish complicity and involvement in the Daesh siege of Kobane are endless here – tour guides and YPG/J militants alike don't shy away from letting it be known how deeply Ankara was involved in support for ISIS at that time. Now the border wall exists, one that for me conjures up images of both the apartheid barrier in Palestine and the 'beautiful wall' promised by President Donald Trump. This fortification keeps Kurdish families apart from one another. But it also cements the idea of Turkey's major worry that the Federal Democratic System of Northern Syria, and Kurdish self-administration, is here to stay.

The scenes along the border in the city's east are indescribable. Burned out cars that were used as mobile explosives by Daesh are everywhere. What were once homes now resemble mostly rubble with the occasional structure and wall still intact. Bullet holes, no doubt, are omnipresent. Occasionally, a seemingly random piece of clothing appears out of nowhere. Apparently, the bodies of killed terrorists are still under the rubble in many places. But miraculously, some families continue to live in this area despite all of the reminders of the horror that once engulfed these streets. This area is now something of a museum – signs all around mark the names of shehids who died street to street. The fighting here was often door to door, or even wall to wall. As our Kurdish friends never hesitate to point out, this wasn't just the scene of the Kurds' battle with ISIS, but the frontline in humanity's war, whether the governments of the so-called international community recognized it or not.

Meeting the Comrades

The next day, we are taken to the YPG/J command centre in the city. Berxwedan seems at first to be an unimposing man, a spirit whose aura of calm and composure gives away little about the previous years of his life. It's impossible to detect how old he is. I think to myself that I wouldn't be surprised to learn that he was in his early twenties, but he could also easily be over the age of 30. As it turns out, he's somewhere right in the middle, a man who has spent just over a quarter of a century on this earth. But the initial sense of mystery that seems to surround him gives way rather quickly when he comes to greet me. It's the way that he embraces me with the most genuine, firm handshake while intensely yet cheerfully looking into my eyes that reveals that despite his relative youthfulness, he's seen far more than the majority of people will ever witness in a lifetime. He has 'that look', one that I've only ever come across a handful of times before. As it turns out, he wasn't supposed to live to even see this age.

After all, the vast majority of his friends passed away sometime in the few months between September 2014 and January 2015, their blood helping to write perhaps the most epic anti-fascist story of the twenty-first century to date.

As we sit down inside the YPG command centre, Berxwedan is soon joined by a woman a few years his junior who goes by the name of Newroz. Their names are suiting, to say the least. Berxwedan means resistance, Newroz the new year. I'm soon drawn by the similarities between these comrades. Their smiles are genuine, no doubt. Yet it becomes impossible to ignore the fact that a part of them is with their fallen friends, physically lost in the struggle against Daesh.

Berxwedan ashes his cigarette and recalls the final days of the battle that saw the so-called Islamic State expelled from this Kurdish city of resistance. He is visibly upset by my question about the so-called 'international community' (led by the US) wanting to claim the glory in this struggle, saying:

The international powers ignored what was taking place here until only a tiny section of the city was still left in our control. Then they intervened at last – not for us in the YPG and YPJ, but for both their geostrategic interests and because they themselves perhaps finally saw the danger Daesh could pose even to them. But we know they didn't give us air support because they actually support our struggle. They certainly don't support us politically. That hasn't changed more than 2 years later.

Newroz chimes in, talking about how the western powers ignoring the battle of Kobane provoked 'a lot of anger'. She also asks, 'How dare they try to take the credit for the liberation of Kobane when they have contributed nothing to the rebuilding of the city?'

A City under Construction

Despite the lack of infrastructure development in some parts of the city, including the eastern part that is being maintained as a museum, Kobane today is a place where rebuilding is palpable.

The day before my meeting with Berxwedan and Newroz, a brand new youth centre opened just streets from where the most intense combat took place during the battle. The youth sang and danced in the streets in front of the new centre before the ribbon was cut to inaugurate a place they'll begin practicing both traditional and modern Kurdish art.

It's symbolic not only that their new home for cultural expression was not so long ago held by the forces of darkness who wanted to rename the city Ayn al-Islam, reflecting their misuse and abuse of Islam (the religion that most Kurds also follow), but also that the centre itself was once a Syrian state institution for culture when the city was officially known as Ayn al-Arab despite it being overwhelmingly Kurdish. The evening of the opening, I meet a man in his late fifties who with tears in his eyes recalls how he used to try coming to the centre in previous decades only to be told, 'You don't belong here.' He was a poor peasant and an 'ignorant Kurd', not one of the assimilated and 'cultured' ones who threw in their lot with the Syrian Arab state. Now he feels overjoyed that his city is free from both Arabization and from Daesh – that it is uniquely Kurdish, that he can walk the streets speaking his native Kurmanji, and that the youth will within days begin the process of both practicing and developing their revolutionary culture within these walls as they have been doing for the past 5 years across the Rojava region.

Elsewhere in the city, homes are being built up and new institutions that house communes, cooperatives and women's organizations spring up with immense vitality. But on the outskirts of the city, a more solemn and sobering kind of construction is taking place. At the cemetery of the shehids, a museum is being built that will remember the 6-month siege of the city and the more than 1,000 hevals who sacrificed their often very brief lives for the freedom of their people. It's this museum that means so much to comrades like Berxwedan and Newroz, since far too many of their friends are buried there.

The Ultimate Sacrifice: Coming to Kobane

As Berxwedan recalls, the decision to come to Kobane was one that didn't need even the most basic thinking over. Like many who came to fight in the city, he is from Bakur (northern Kurdistan) within the present day borders of Turkey. He says that for his group of 24 friends who decided to cross the border, coming to defend the people of Kobane felt like a basic duty. He knew the risk of death was massive, as is evidenced by the fact that today only four of the group are still alive including him. For Newroz, a native of the Rojava region, of her group of ten comrades (five men and five women), only four remain alive today. Two are missing their legs. Only her and one other heval are able-bodied and continue to serve in the YPJ. Berxwedan puts into one sentence the level of sacrifice that coming to Kobane entailed: 'There are many stories of those crossing the border from Turkey at night. They came over, were divided into units and went straight into battle. Many of these comrades didn't live to see the sunrise the next day in Rojava.'

It's these words that stay in my head for hours, for days, for weeks. Probably in all earnest, they will linger in my mind for a lifetime. At the shehid cemetery, I was struck by the birth years of so many of the fallen. 1995, 1996, 1997. It feels haunting to an outsider, but I was impressed, even a bit confused, at how Berxwedan and Newroz seemed to retain their calm in recalling such stories. That evening after leaving their company, I speak to one of my fellow internationalists about something we both noticed – our hesitation to ask certain questions that we were afraid might trigger painful or tragic memories, and their complete willingness to discuss any subject. I think of war veterans I know from the US, for instance, who shy away from talking about the experiences in wars abroad. Perhaps it was out of shame, we both suggest. Maybe, though, it also has something to do with the collective nature of the society that is being built and defended in Rojava. The next day, we got at least part of that answer.

Institute for the Families of the Shehids

Just as the smiles of Berxwedan and Newroz don't necessarily give away the extent of the struggle and torment they have been through, neither do the faces of the dozen or so members of the institute that handles the work related to the families of the shehids who I am fortunate enough to meet with on one of my mornings in Kobane. The institute is called Saziya Malbaten Sehiden in Kurmanji. All of those who work here have lost sons or daughters to the war over the past 5 years since self-administration was proclaimed. At this centre in the heart of the city, the bodies of the fallen YPG and YPJ comrades still pass through on what seems like an almost daily basis. They are prepared here for burial, but the main work of the institute begins after this, in making sure that the families of the comrades are taken care of in light of their passing. Currently, there are 300 wives of shehids and 1,000 children who receive services from the institution. As they point out, these families are not just Kurdish, but are also Arab, Assyrian and Armenian, reflective of the multi-ethnic composition of this region of Syria.

As we sit outback in the courtyard of the centre and discuss concepts related to internationalism and how important it is that leftists and socialists from around the world come to Rojava to witness and take part in the revolution, one of my fellow foreigners proceeds to ask about the issue of psychology and mental health in light of the tragedy of war and loss that people in Syria deal with constantly. The answers are not really forthcoming – not because they don't want to deal with the question, but because the question, which is one I also had, contains in it strong elements of western and individualistic ways of thinking. It somewhat confuses our Rojavan friends. In our self-centred societies, we often rely on such services perhaps almost exclusively in the place of strong, organic community support networks. But as one of our friends tells us, here the society is deeply communal and becoming more so through the revolution. Therefore, although a centre for psychology has just opened in Kobane, the men and women who work at the institute know little about it. It's the daily work that they do with the families of martyrs that takes priority in helping them cope, in addition to the sense of societal inclusion in all aspects of democratic decision making that is being developed here. These are the primary ways that mental wellness is taken care of and enhanced.

A practical way that this communal society manifests becomes clear when a constantly smiling man in his late fifties, Heval Gelhat, begins speaking about his son who died in the past year in battle:

> I got the news that my son had become a shehid. The other
> members of the committee here said that it was too close to
> home, that they should take care of his funeral instead of me.
> But no! How could I not fulfil my duty to him when I have
> done so hundreds of times for others who have given their
> lives for our new society?

His sentiments are echoed by another story told by a woman
about a funeral that she attended last year. The father of this
YPG shehid was standing there without a single tear in his eye.
The woman later asked him why he hadn't cried. He said he
hadn't cried at any funerals before for the other YPG and YPJ
comrades, then said plainly, 'Were those young men and women
not also my own children?'

I feel overwhelmed with the strength of these fathers
and mothers at this point. After all, every single one of the
members of the committee who I am in the presence of have
lost children to this war of anti-fascism. After a short, somewhat
uncomfortable pause, another opens his mouth and says, 'This is
our revolutionary approach to death.'

Serkeftin (To the Victory of the Struggle)

Back to Berxwedan and the YPG command centre. He recalls a
story about wall to wall combat during the battle in late 2014. He
speaks of being five comrades strong in a room and being able
to hear Daesh taking a sledgehammer to a wall only separated
from them by one other wall in the same building.

'Fortunately for us, we had a small hole in the wall so as soon
as they knocked down the wall they had been working on for
what seemed like forever, we threw grenades over and killed
them all.' He lets out a massive laugh as punctuation to his latest
war story. It's not that Berxwedan or his comrades are blood

thirsty or find amusement in tales of death and destruction. But clearly in the horrors of war, victories like this were cause for a deep, nervous sigh of relief – and for temporary celebration.

What's tangible in stories like these is that there is a deep love for not only 'his people' but for all of humanity and basic democratic sentiments. As he explained, 'With every Daesh member killed, we knew we were a step closer to our children being able to grow up free and not as slaves, or worse. We knew this struggle wasn't just for Kurds, but for all Syrians and all people.'

Newroz echoes his words, saying, 'you have to understand that the YPG and YPJ are not aggressive military structures. This is what separates us from the other forces in Syria, the so-called "rebels". We are a movement of revenge, yes. But we are defensive, not aggressive. We are just trying to defend our people.'

Both Newroz and Berxwedan continue their service in the YPG/J, more than 2 years after the battle of Kobane concluded. At this time, the assault on Raqqa had just started. I was curious as to what was to come next for both of them. Their answers seemed somewhat choreographed, but by this point in Rojava I had learned that if it appeared that way to me, it's most likely because of my western individualistic prejudices, not because they are somehow lying to uphold the 'party line'.

Newroz said matter-of-factly, 'We'll contribute whatever we can to this revolution. Maybe it's on the frontlines. Maybe it's in talking to people like you. But what we're doing is bigger than ourselves.'

It's now well past dusk, and our meeting has already gone on far longer than expected. I'm eager to leave by now, not because I want to leave the company of such beautiful comrades, but because frankly I don't know how to really process the extent of the stories I've heard from them over the last 7 plus hours.

In customary revolutionary Kurdish fashion, I embrace both

of them with a 'serkeftin', translated roughly as 'to the victory of the struggle'. I have just met two people who in western phraseology, I might refer to as real living heroes. In Rojava, however, there are countless Berxwedans and Newrozes. I feel somewhat ashamed to leave. I have called myself a revolutionary for years, but my extent of commitment could never rival what these comrades have showed me is necessary for the success of a true liberation struggle. I leave the two of them, but without exaggeration and at the risk of sounding immensely cliched, the two of them could never leave me.

Leaving Kobane

A few days later, I leave not just the comrades but all of Kobane behind. My week in this city of resistance has changed me beyond recognition. I think of my entire life, including of course my life in politics, and where I need to be headed in the period ahead. Something profound was stirring inside of me on the way here, and now that I am leaving it is even more pronounced.

But this trip to Kobane wasn't quite over yet. On the outskirts of the city after leaving, we made a quick stop at a place that had been used – depending on your point of origin – as either the starting point or end of a tunnel that once connected Rojava and Bakur. The comrades used to send resources across the border through this tunnel, but it was most recently used by Daesh when they took control of this area. It's now been sealed shut, but a memory of the war has been left behind – the skeleton of a Daesh member is apparent under a stack of rubble just inside the cave that leads to the now defunct tunnel. Outside, Kurdish children play carelessly as a shepherd smiles at us, struggling to control his restless sheep. I think of just how dramatically different life was here just a little over 2 years ago. The smile of that man, the playfulness of those children, has only been made possible through the sacrifice of the Berxwedans and the Newrozes, as well as their countless friends whose blood has nourished the soil here. I think of how somehow, someway, I hope that one day I can give even a fraction to the defence of humanity that they have sacrificed.

Chapter 3

YPG and YPJ: Revolutionists or Pawns of the Empire?

'The YPJ', types Becky the Western, 'anti-imperialist' feminist 'should have chosen a dignified beheading, gang rape and massacres of all women, the Kurds and the peoples of north Syria rather than choose to accept weapons from the filthy imperialists to defend themselves against ISIS!!!.' Her finger smashes the exclamation mark button to add emphasis to her point as she takes a delicate sip from her soy milk Strawberries and Creme Frappuccino before commencing retyping on her ipad 7. 'I would have definitely supported them then! but certainly not now!' She glares at the Mexican waitress who places her order of Camembert and Mascarpone Blueberry Cheesecake for interrupting her ground breaking political analysis of Syria. Outside the rain pours buckets as she sits cozy and comfortable in a corner in her local Starbucks cafe. She briefly ignores her iphone, which suddenly beeps reminding her to reschedule her hot yoga class so as to not clash with her pet poodle's appointment at the dog salon. She concludes her status, accompanied with a self satisfied smirk, with the line 'Even sexual slavery in the streets of Raqqa and Aleppo would have been better than weapons from imperialists! That is the kind of feminism that I support from Brown, Muslim, Black and Indigenous women of the world!'
Kurdish activist Hawzhin Azeez

It seems like the paradox of all paradoxes. The US and its western allies are engaged in a ruthless and relentless war against the Syrian government in Damascus, one that has seen the so-called defenders of democracy and freedom support some of the most vile and reactionary terror organizations the world has seen in recent history. President Donald Trump recently intervened militarily for the first time against the government forces with a barrage of cruise missiles that had the effect of aiding groups that ideologically operate in the same vein as al-Qaeda in the country's north-west.

No, it isn't *this* that's the ultimate paradox. After all, US support for groups linked to or in the mould of Salafi and Wahhabi extremism is nothing new at all, lest one forget their support for the so-called Mujahideen in Afghanistan in the 1980s. What is far more paradoxical is that the US has been providing military support in northern Syria for a group that not only isn't reactionary, not only claims to be socialist and feminist, but actually has ideological ties to the Kurdistan Workers' Party (PKK), the same organization that has been at war with NATO's second largest army in Turkey for more than 3 decades.

The fact that the Democratic Union Party (PYD) and its armed components, the YPG and YPJ, are leading a genuine social revolution amidst the chaos in Syria is without question. The month I spent travelling across the areas that are under their control was more than enough time to convince me that this revolutionary experiment that is taking place is truly unique, beyond imaginative and has a sweeping democratic and socialist character.

I was continuously impressed with what I witnessed there, from the commune structures and the cooperatives, to the women's organizations and the thriving arts and culture academies. I was struck by the way in which the movement was honest and straight forward about the many contradictions that are emerging in the course of the process of radically transforming society. I can also truly say that for the first time in my life, despite all my travels to countries that have been engaged in some level of socialist construction (Venezuela, Cuba and North Korea), I truly felt like I was seeing the kind of vitality and deeply democratic, grassroots society I had always imagined could – and should – come to life.

The greatest contradiction was never far from my mind, though. It often felt perturbing. I couldn't understand what to make of what the YPG/J calls its 'tactical military cooperation' with the US. After all, to one who has come of age politically in the school of revolutionary Marxism and anti-imperialism, I was taught to not touch anything that comes even slightly close to the hand of the Pentagon or Central Intelligence Agency (CIA) – and for good reason. After all, the US is not exactly in the habit of supporting genuine revolutions anywhere on the face of the planet.

Concluding that indeed the so-called Rojava project is a genuine social revolution inside of what I have long viewed as a US-backed regime-change operation against a government in Damascus that has refused to play by the rules of global neo-liberalism, I felt the desperate need to have my questions answered on some level: Is it that the YPG and YPJ are merely using the US? On the flipside, is the US merely using the YPG and YPJ? Are these Kurds objectively doing little more than aiding US imperialism when looking at the bigger picture? Is US imperialism, due to the complexities of the war, actually knowingly aiding a socialist revolutionary process? Or is the truth somewhere in between? Are elements contained in every possible answer, or is the answer not even one that can necessarily be made clear yet? Better yet, are my questions even fair, or do they contain in them evidence of western prejudice and privilege?

During and After Kobane

It was in the final stages of the push of the YPG and YPJ in Kobane in early 2015 that the US-led coalition finally – under tremendous international pressure – agreed to support the Kurdish forces with airstrikes to push back the so-called Islamic State. To this day, the US is never shy about asserting how important it views its role as having been in the liberation of Kobane, though my encounters with YPG/J fighters in that city recently taught me they don't exactly view it the same way. Their overall sentiment expressed to me about the US role was one of anger for not having intervened sooner and turning a blind eye to the suffering of the people at the hands of Daesh. This was enough to convince them that their intervention was only made for their own geostrategic objectives, and not out of genuine support for the YPG/J.

The words of Kurdish activist and academic Dilar Dirik are important to digest. She recently wrote an article in *ROAR Magazine* entitled 'Radical Democracy: The Frontline Against Fascism' that took up the question of the inability of substantial parts of the western left to lend support to the YPG/J, especially in the aftermath of US air support during the siege of Kobane.

The public image of the armed forces of Rojava shifted abruptly in the eyes of sections of the left after the liberation of Kobane. While this was undeniably a historic battle, won by an organized community and the power of free women, the widespread sympathy crumbled the very moment that forces on the ground received aerial support from the US-led coalition. Having long been among the most aggrieved victims of imperialism in the Middle East, the Kurds and their neighbors did not require any further enlightenment about the evils of empire. The genocides and massacres committed against them through collaborations of imperialist forces are still in living memory. Dogmatic, binary worldviews and narrow-minded criticisms do not propose any viable alternatives for people fighting for their lives on the ground. More importantly, they do not save lives.

Military Support – but Not Political

It's now been well over 2 years since the fascists were driven from Kobane, and the US continues to support the Kurdish forces and their extended military umbrella known as the Syrian Democratic Forces (SDF), with the Trump administration giving the green light in early May for these forces to receive heavy weapons. The SDF largely consists of Arab militias who are also fighting for the establishment of democratic structures, inspired by the successes of the poly-ethnic and commune-based administrations set up in northern Syria to date.

The US has not only started the process of providing heavy weaponry to the SDF, but there are nearly 1,000 US special forces operating on the ground alongside them in addition to a deployment of marines. Are these groups within the SDF merely the new counter-revolutionary proxy organizations that the US has hedged its bets on in light of the collapse of the reactionary Free Syrian Army (FSA) groups that Turkey seems hell bent on resuscitating?

It may not provide a full answer to the question, but it's important to note that while the US *militarily* supports the SDF's push on Daesh's capital Raqqa under the banner of Operation Wrath of the Euphrates, Washington has done everything possible to keep the PYD – the political arm of the YPG/J – away from the negotiating table at the Geneva peace talks. Also, the federal system that has been set up by the PYD and Rojava's Movement for a Democratic Society (TEV-DEM) has received no sort of support or hint of consideration from the US, which has continuously stressed that 'ad hoc federalism' is not something that is encouraged by Washington.

Running often contrary to the stance of the US on Rojava has been the position of Russia. While Moscow is usually thought of as the military muscle coming to the aid of the Ba'athist government, it is also the Russians who have most recently proposed a new constitution for Syria based at least in part on the federalization advocated by the PYD and reflective of the country's multi-ethnic character (hence suggesting changing the name of the country from the Syrian Arab Republic to simply

Syrian Republic). Russia has also advocated that the PYD be included in the third round of Geneva talks, a proposal that was shot down by the US. In addition, the first office of the PYD abroad was opened in Moscow in February 2016, and it has been the Russian state that has facilitated talks between the Syrian government and PYD on what a settlement might look like that would allow for peace between the forces of both sides. Most recently, Russia has joined in the quest to work militarily with the YPG/J, establishing a base to train forces of the Kurdish units and the SDF in Afrin in late March, as well as creating a buffer zone there to prevent Turkish forces from launching attacks on them. Therefore, it appears that perhaps Moscow has hedged its bets on the continued success of not only the military forces of Rojava, but of the success of its political project and its endurance.

Ideological Enemies

The practical and basic necessity of survival is more than enough to explain why the YPG/J would accept military cooperation with the US. This is what I have heard some western keyboard warriors and armchair activists dismiss in an over simplistic manner as 'dancing with the Devil'. After all, why would revolutionary socialists otherwise team up with the US, unless of course they aren't really revolutionaries at all? My observations have led me to believe that these forces are, in fact, genuine revolutionists.

Throughout my trip, I was fascinated to see if I could detect varying opinions within the ranks of the YPG or the political organizations about how to assess this cooperation with the US through its Operation Inherent Resolve, the official name for the so-called coalition's anti-Daesh operations. What do these radicals make of the motives of Washington, whether under the administration of Barack Obama or that of Donald Trump, to work side by side with them?

A YPG commander, Cihan Kendal, said early in 2017 in an interview with *Plan C* that, 'America would like to have us as a main ally, but they know that is not possible; militarily we are cooperating at times, but ideologically we are enemies.' It's a sentiment that Cihan repeated to me when I met him in northern Syria. As he told me, 'We are engaged in a democratic revolution, but this revolution is also being led by a socialist party, so of course it is a socialist revolution, too. So naturally, this is something the US would never support.'

Another YPG commander who I meet in Kobane doesn't hold back, telling me:

> There are those who say because we are tactically cooperating with the US that this isn't a real revolution. But tell me, how are we supposed to defeat ISIS and defend our revolution without heavy weapons? We know that they will give us weapons to take Raqqa, but at the same time they don't even want us to govern Raqqa our own way. We know that once their strategic objectives are achieved, they will abandon us.

On another occasion just days later, I am fortunate enough to meet with yet another impressive ideologue who reveals to me that he and his comrades have a very extensive knowledge of the history of revolutionary movements. On the wall behind him is a portrait of Abdullah Ocalan. Below it hangs one of Vladimir Lenin speaking to the masses in Petrograd in 1917. He points to the portrait of Lenin and says, 'Here's a man who one hundred years ago accepted a bulletproof train from the imperialist German state to head home to Russia and wage the Bolshevik revolution. Do we view him today as an agent of German imperialism?' Of course, whether or not the comparison is completely apt is a question in and of itself, but the point from the commander isn't lost. He has told me as clearly as he possibly can: we aren't some pawns or puppets of the US. We are revolutionaries first and foremost.

Ultra-Leftist Opportunists? Or Real Revolutionaries?

Although the question of how the military cooperation between the world's most bloodthirsty superpower and the world's most radical revolutionaries will end up is far from settled at this point, it would be absurd to think that the revolutionaries in the Kurdish Freedom Movement, who have 4 decades of experience combating these same imperialists, have suddenly forgotten about their sins. Some on the western left may just dismiss the YPG/J as ultra-leftists who are opportunistically joining forces with the empire. After having spent some time in Rojava, I think that assessment doesn't in the least bit correspond to reality.

It's necessary to reflect deeper on the words of Dilar Dirk in her recent article:

> For the people whose families were being massacred by ISIS, the ease with which Western leftists seemed to advocate for the rejection of military aid in favor of romantic notions of revolutionary purity, were incomprehensible to say the least. Advocacy of unconditional anti-imperialism, detached from real human existence and concrete realities, is a luxury that those far removed from the trauma of war can afford. Well-aware of the dangers of being instrumentalized only to be abandoned by great powers like the US and Russia, but stuck between a rock and a hard place, the priority of the SDF was — and remains — to first of all survive and eliminate the most immediate threats to the existence of hundreds of thousands of people across the vast stretches of territory it controls.

Dirik's writing struck a chord with me upon my return to Europe from Syria. It's incredibly easy – shamefully so in some ways – to sit in the comfort of our western homes and criticize the 'sell out' nature of a movement for 'collaborating' with imperialism when the lives of so many are literally on the line. However, once one actually takes the time to investigate the reality on the ground and what the forces of the YPG/J are up against, including being blockaded by Turkey, Daesh and the narrow nationalists of the Kurdistan Democratic Party (KDP) in Iraq, a different picture should emerge.

Armchair revolutionism and solidarity contingent only on notions of 'purity' is meaningless in the real world. Looking at the region – and the world – as nothing more than a chessboard can easily lead to adopting the politics of 'the enemy of my enemy is my friend', which is deeply flawed, lazy and can lead to support for extremely reactionary movements while foregoing support for those that actually advance the same kind of politics we would like to see in our own countries.

The words of the second of the YPG commanders I encountered and addressed my concerns about the US to resonated the most with me when travelling home. As he put it:

It's of course useful to us that Trump would send us a couple of Humvees. This definitely helps in our fight against Daesh. But let's remember that one F-16 sold by Trump to Turkey could take out all these vehicles in a second. We know which side the US will ultimately pick if it has to, and it won't be ours.

Chapter 4

'The Kurds': Internationalists or Narrow Nationalists?

It seems impossible. I look down from the hilltop that I'm standing on to see a very narrow stretch of river. From here, it appears as rather insignificant. This, I'm told, is the mighty Tigris, and on the other side of it lays Iraq. Where I stand is Syria, the war-torn country that has already endured 6 years of destruction up to this point. To some in my company this particular region is more frequently called Rojava, but to the even more politically correct of comrades the name Democratic Federal System of Northern Syria is used.

Looking down at the calm of the river ahead of me, I'm amazed. I had crossed this border a couple of weeks before, but this is the first time I'm seeing it during daylight. When I had crossed over, I realized that the flow of traffic – all lorries – was completely one-sided, travelling in the direction of Iraq. However, it was late at night and I was eager to see what this looked like during the day.

Well, here I was, and the volume of traffic wasn't much higher at all. To be exact, I counted a sum total of zero cars making their way between the two countries over the half hour I stood there taking in the gorgeous scenery. There were a few more lorries than I had remembered seeing the last time around, but I knew one thing for sure – this was no ordinary border crossing.

This was a border that previously had been administered by the rival Ba'ath governments in both countries, but was now manned on both sides by Kurdish administrations. Yet the character of those two governing structures couldn't be more different, to such a degree that the Iraqi side under the control of the KDP had decided to enact a full embargo and blockade against what was then called Rojava on 19 March 2016. It was now just about a year later, and the embargo hadn't been eased at all. There is no business as usual here.

A Kurdish-Imperialist Project?

A few days later, I'm sitting in Qamishlo, the de-facto capital of the democratic self-administration of northern Syria. I'm trying to make sense of the dozens of pages of notes I've taken over the past few days while visiting civil society organizations, and while taking a break to catch up on the news in the rest of the world, I stumble across an article that a few of my Facebook friends have re-posted about how there is an imperialist project to establish a 'Greater Kurdistan' in Iraq and Syria.

It actually makes no difference which particular article I'm referring to. There are quite a few pieces that have been written on the topic which all more or less conform to the same thesis. I let out a chuckle at just seeing the headline, but once I get into the content of the article I'm not as amused. I think to myself that this kind of lazy analysis is all too common, and that it's unfortunate that it finds traction among those who should frankly be a bit more investigative before publishing such theories.

To be sure, if there's one person who can understand the perspective of some self-proclaimed anti-imperialists who view the question of Kurdish self-determination as being almost entirely wrapped up with the machinations of the US and the western powers in the Middle East, it's myself.

The first time I visited Basur (southern Kurdistan, or northern Iraq) was in the early months of 2013. I came as a journalist who had the task of putting together a series of video stories about the development of the Kurdistan Regional Government, now operating at what appeared to be near independence from the central Baghdad government. I arrived in Erbil, or Hewler as the Kurds refer to it. Here, capitalist modernity with its influx of Turkish and US capital was omnipresent in the new shopping malls and luxury housing developments. I stayed in the country for no longer than a week, and barely had the time to grasp the differences between the KDP that controlled Erbil and the Patriotic Union of Kurdistan (PUK) that governed in Sulaymaniyah, let alone to understand what was taking place across the border in northern Syria.

It was my own inability to engage in the art of investigation, but it was also a stubbornness when it came to not daring to challenge my preconceptions of the Middle East in light of the US wars of aggression that began in 2003 with the invasion of Iraq. The way I saw it, the US had for a decade been engaged in the attempt to overthrow a number of states in the region, such as Iraq and Syria, Libya and Iran, and needless to say in those conquests imperialism was more than thrilled to use the shortcomings of the targeted governments (many times the national question and very real oppression of ethnic minorities) to facilitate its goal of regime change. No doubt this was the case in Iraq, where the KDP and PUK both took part in the US campaign against the Ba'ath government, leading the PUK's leader, Jalal Talabani, to become president of the country in 2005. As a result, my logic when it came to the idea that there was a Kurdish entity forming in northern Syria – another state targeted for regime change by my government – could only be that this was a new KRG that was emerging.

Therefore, I believe I understand almost completely the perspective of the western anti-imperialists who have been weary of the Syrian Kurdish polity that has developed since 2012 under the banner of the Rojava Revolution. After all, this weariness and scepticism was a major part of my position for several years before I made the decision to commit to a deeper level of investigation. What I've found, both through research and through my trip to the areas under control of the federation, is that there are some very basic misconceptions of the Kurdish question in Iraq and Syria that need to be addressed. Here are some of the fundamentals:

1. **'The Kurds' Do Not Have an Identity of Political Positions**

   'The Kurds'. This has been one of the most troubling expressions that is used not only in the mainstream media, but also by a number of so-called leftists. It's as if the entirety of the region can somehow be lumped together as one people with a single position on what should become of the area known historically as Kurdistan. The reality is far different, as the tensions between the KDP and the Rojava self-administration under the leadership of the Democratic Union Party (PYD) show, or even within Iraq where the KDP and PUK are currently at loggerheads over how to deal with the Syrian federal system (the PUK has been more supportive of Rojava than the KDP, for instance). There are conservative Kurdish parties and social-democratic ones that have political orientations that gel well with imperialism, and there are at the same time organizations that have revolutionary and socialist politics that cannot possibly be reconciled – at the least in the long-run – with western interests. This is fundamental and important to grasp.

2. **The Narrow Nationalism of Barzani's KDP Plays Well With Imperialism**

   The KDP under the leadership of Masoud Barzani can be said to have an orientation that is representative of the comprador-bourgeoisie in Iraqi Kurdish society. Here, feudal tradition is combined with the glitz and glamour of the ascendancy of capitalist development. It is none other than the Turkish government of President Recep Tayyip Erdogan that has had the cosiest of relationships with Barzani and the KDP. While Erdogan is engaged in a ruthless war within the borders of Turkey against the Kurdish population there, he welcomed Barzani to Istanbul in late February, affording him the red carpet treatment as the flag of the KRG flew at the airport.

Despite the fact that Turkey opposed the Kurdish region's independence referendum that was carried out on 25 September 2017, threatening military action alongside Iran and Iraq's central government, the importance of Turkish capital in the KRG remains significant.

3. **Democratic Confederalism is a Break with the Nation-State**

By contrast with the narrow nationalist and capitalist orientation of Barzani, the Kurdish Freedom Movement that is grouped around the Kurdistan Communities Union (Koma Civaken Kurdistan, or KCK) have a radically different perspective on how the region should be organized. The KCK functions as an umbrella for all of the parties in the four parts of historic Kurdistan that follow the theoretical positions developed by Abdullah Ocalan, the founder of the Kurdistan Workers' Party (PKK) in Turkey. The other groups in the KCK today are the PYD (Democratic Union Party) that leads Syria's revolution in the north, the PJAK (Kurdistan Free Life Party) that operates in Iran, and PCDK (Kurdistan Democratic Solution Party) which organizes in Iraq.

The PKK and Ocalan considered themselves as part of the international communist movement from the time that the party was founded in 1978 and the armed struggle against the Turkish state began in 1984. However, in the aftermath of Ocalan's imprisonment in 1999 and the crisis of international Marxism, Ocalan began to critically reflect on the concept of how national liberation could truly be achieved. In his transformed views on the question, he began to see the nation-state as being insufficient, and even oppressive in its very nature. As he saw it, there was the possibility that a 'free Kurdistan' would create the same problems for other oppressed ethnic groups (Armenians, Assyrians and so on) as the Turkish Republic had for the Kurdish population. Therefore, he developed a new paradigm, announced in 2005, that advocated for a non-state, libertarian socialism in which local assemblies would be the basis of a new power.

4. **Rojava's Revolutionaries Are Not Separatists**
The PYD, as part of the KCK, upholds this ideology of democratic confederalism. Organized in 2003, 5 years after Ocalan left Syria and 4 years after his arrest in Kenya, the PYD had to compete in the Rojava region for political support with the other Kurdish parties that had traditionally organized in Ba'athist Syria, namely the Syrian branch of the KDP, known as KDP-S. In 2012, the PYD positioned itself to be able to take advantage of the chaos of the war in Syria to declare autonomous self-government in the majority Kurdish areas.

Contrary to the view often incorrectly expressed that holds that these revolutionaries are separatists, the ideology and practice of the so-called democratic self-administration since 2012 has been very different. There has never been the slightest hint that the region could declare independence, and documents such as the Social Contract have made clear that the areas under PYD and Movement for Democratic Society (TEV-DEM) control are and will remain a part of Syria.

In fact, even the word 'Rojava' (meaning 'west' in Kurdish) has been officially removed from use and replaced with 'Democratic Federal System of Northern Syria' (DFSNS) as of late 2016. The reason is clear: such an expression as 'Rojava' is Kurdish-centric, and will only help to create long-term tensions between Kurds and the other ethnic groups of the region such as Arabs, Assyrians, Turkmen, Armenians and others.

5. **The Relationship of the KDP and ENKS to the DFSNS is One of Hostility**

Not only has the PYD been staunchly opposed to such a move to separate from the rest of Syria, but in 2011 it was one of the founding members of the National Coordination Committee for Democratic Change (NCB), a group of political parties that many members of the Syrian National Council and other Arab-dominated opposition organizations declared to be an 'Assadist' internal opposition.

Whether these allegations have any merit is the topic for another discussion entirely, but what's most noteworthy about the NCB is that it initially included a number of other Kurdish parties. However, these parties soon left to establish another umbrella organization, the Kurdish National Council (Encumena Nistimani ya Kurdi li Suriye, or ENKS). ENKS is funded by Masoud Barzani and functions as the primary internal opposition to the democratic self-administration in northern Syria.

The relationship is tumultuous to say the least. The same day that I crossed from Iraq into Syria, the military wing of ENKS, known as Rojava Peshmerga, attacked the KCK-linked Shengal Resistance Units (YBS) in Shengal (otherwise known as Mount Singar). The terrible political calculations of Barzani for such a move cannot be overstated. It was Shengal that came to international attention in late 2014 as the fascist forces of Daesh were engaged in massacres of the Yezidi population there. The PKK was the primary force that facilitated the liberation of Shengal from Daesh, and in the aftermath the YBS was set up as a self-defence organization for the people there.

Just over 2 years on, here was Barzani using weapons provided by Germany to attack the very people who defended this land from the forces of darkness. It was a political move that both showed subservience to Turkey and revealed clearly that the interests of the Barzani ideologies and Apoists (those who advocate Abdullah Ocalan's position could not be more different.

6. **A Greater Kurdistan Is Incompatible with the Rojava Revolution**

It's worth noting that while the US and the YPG/J coordinate their efforts militarily in northern Syria, there has been no political support forthcoming from the US towards the PYD. Time and time again, the PYD has been sidelined from the Geneva peace talks, and in November 2016, Deputy Spokesperson for the Department of State Mark Toner said of the prospect of a federal Syria:

> We don't want to see any kind of ad hoc federalism or federalist system arise. We don't want to see semi-autonomous zones. The reality is, though, as territory is liberated from Daesh, you got to get some kind of governance back into these areas, but by no means are we condoning or – any kind of, as I said, ad hoc semi-autonomous areas in northern Syria.

That being said, the idea that the US and western powers would like to see the balkanization of the region is hardly beyond the stretch of the imagination. The carving up of the Middle East into statelets that can be easily managed and which would be too weak to put up any substantial resistance to the penetration of foreign capital seems a sensible task if you're sitting in the halls of power in Washington or London.

However, finding the forces who are willing to go to bat for you in a political way on the ground is something much more complicated. Barzani and his KDP have proved their loyalty to this imperialist project over recent decades, despite differing opinions on the 25 September referendum.

Yet, the idea that the socialists who find themselves forging a revolutionary path in northern Syria – who have a vastly different concept of how to organize society – could be partners just as loyal seems to lack the prospect of coming to fruition. Washington is obviously nervous about what the idea of a new radical society such as Rojava can represent in the region, and for this reason the buck stops at limited military support.

Chapter 5

The Centrality of Women's Liberation in Northern Syria (Theory)

After the first week I spent in northern Syria had come and gone, a friend of mine in the US sent me an animated text message to check up on me: 'Yo! How's it's going out there??! You staying safe??'

Where to even begin was the question. There was so much I wanted to tell him at that moment about what had already been such a life-changing first 7 or 8 days, but I knew I wouldn't be able to convey a great deal in both the limited amount of time I had to reply (wi-fi wasn't always so easy to find while on the road) and the fact that a text isn't exactly the best way to communicate profound emotions related to witnessing such monumental social change (there's no emojis for those revolutionary concepts that I know of that can do justice). My mind raced as I thought back over the days that felt like weeks, the week that felt like a year. Then, after about 20 seconds of thinking it over, I simply wrote back: 'Man, it's amazing. A deep social revolution. Women really do run things here.'

Well, that may have been a bit of an oversimplification. If anything, I blame our reliance on technology in which ideas have to be greatly compacted for any reductionism that comes with the sentiments expressed. Women of course do not 'run things' in Rojava – it's not as if the society has been turned upside down, especially overnight, so that a deeply patriarchal society has now become a matriarchal one (nor is that the goal). Also, I wasn't trying to romanticize the revolution, or to fall into the trap (which I will try my best not to do here in my writing) to be just another western man to somehow fetishize the role of women in the Kurdish military struggle, as so much of our mainstream press has done with its portrayal of the women of the YPJ.

Still, the point I was trying to make to my friend maintains its validity: the Rojava Revolution is fundamentally, at its core, about the liberation of women from the shackles of patriarchal degradation that is wrapped up, and inherent, in capitalism.

First Impressions of the Central Role of Women in the Struggle

It didn't take long after my arrival in Rojava to see this concept in action. The first place I arrived at once crossing the border from Iraq into northern Syria was a military checkpoint that was guarded by women of the Asayish, or security of the democratic self-administration (I very nearly typed '*manned* by women' here, which would have made for an embarrassing, and maybe revealing error about the kind of language we are often naturally driven to employ). It was difficult to comprehend that just a few hundred kilometres from this point, the fascist forces of Daesh still held the city of Raqqa and a considerable amount of territory in which women are confined to a life of slavery and drudgery.

After hours later arriving in the city of Qamishlo, I was told that the first order of business for me and the group of internationalists I was with was going to be to sit through a series of educationals to get a better sense of the foundations of the revolution that had been started half a decade before (as I was to find out, this process has actually been ongoing for several decades). These would focus on what they deem to be key concepts, including the history of the Kurdish Freedom Movement, internationalism and the women's struggle. The classes on the women's movement were to be divided into two sessions, one focusing on the history of the Kurdish women's movement and one on the 'science of women', referred to in Kurmanji as 'Jineologi'.

The seriousness with which the comrades presented the

education on the fundamental role of women in transforming society in the four parts of Kurdistan (that has now extended to Arab cities and villages that have been liberated by the YPG/J-led SDF) showed me very clearly that in this struggle, women's emancipation was no mere footnote, or something that was alluded to but which lagged behind in practice.

I had known before coming to Syria that the Kurdish movement in both Turkey (or as Kurdish regions there are called, Bakur) and in Rojava practises a system of co-chairs, in which for every man elected to hold an office, a woman also has to be selected. I knew that there was a system of autonomous organization for women, of which the YPJ was but one example. But I was curious to really dive into understanding just what this official organizational structure meant in tangible terms. Before seeing it in practice, however, the educationals provided a necessary framework for understanding how it was that this revolution was even made possible to begin with.

Making Women's Liberation a Priority in the Kurdish Freedom Movement

If you get your only information about the world from the western mainstream media, you might be forgiven for believing that the reason why the Rojava Revolution has been able to see women actively fighting on the frontlines against the so-called Islamic State is because 'the Kurds' have something inherent in them that allows this to be possible. Mainstream narratives seem to soft peddle, if not overly make the argument, that by their nature 'the Kurds' are more predisposed to gender equality than others in the region, especially Arabs. Of course, another element to the mainstream western press giving airtime to the role of the YPJ in the Syrian war is that it plays well with the establishment's peddling of Islamophobia, especially to equate Daesh with Islam, and mischaracterize the YPJ and 'the Kurds' as being the vanguard of a kind of secularism that is 'western' in orientation (you would be hard-pressed to find reports that mention the fact that the majority of Kurds are Sunni Muslims).

The reason that a series of classes for internationalists arriving in Rojava on the history of the Kurdish women's movement is so essential is to provide a corrective for the kind of misconceptions brought forward by our beloved establishment news outlets. The reality is that far from 'the Kurds' having gender equality in their genes (one can look at Iraqi Kurdistan today to make the opposite argument), the groundwork for the YPJ and every women's organization in northern Syria today has been laid by the more than 40 years of the Kurdish Freedom Movement organizing the people.

The Long View of History

The hevals were keen to point out that if one takes the long view of history, the system of patriarchal oppression may at most comprise 2 per cent of it, as various examples of social organization and ways of living preceded the 'sexual ruptures' that gave rise to men's dominant position in society that we often think of as being somehow natural. Even to this day, evidence of these previous societies in Mesopotamia, some of them matriarchal, can still be seen in many mountainous regions of Kurdistan that were less susceptible to foreign invasions, thus allowing the communities to maintain their 'natural' beliefs (the Yezidis are one example of this).

To the revolutionaries in Kurdistan, it's insufficient to simply talk about the heroines of today or even of the past 4 decades. The examples given of women resisting patriarchy in the Middle East start much further back than one might expect. Nefertiti's resistance to the priests and the pharaoh in 300 BC is cited alongside examples such as Queen Zenobia's refusal to go along with Roman dictates in Palmyra in the third century. After the first division of Kurdistan, Xanimzade led the tribal resistance to the massacres committed by the Persian Empire, and she was followed by names such as Halime Xanim, who resisted the rule of the Ottoman Empire.

The examples of twentieth-century Kurdish women who are the modern forerunners to women in the YPJ are seemingly without end. Adile Xanim helped bring together 56 tribes in a confederation in modern day Iran before her death in 1924. Zarife (1882-1937) was a widely known leader among the Alevi population who was executed due to a traitor giving her in to the Turkish authorities. The same year during the uprising of the Kurdish people in Dersim, a woman named Bese, who had led an uprising, threw herself from the rocks to avoid capture. In the next decade, women like Gulazer and Mina Xanim would play a key role in the establishment of the first Kurdish socialist state, the short-lived Mahabad Republic (1946).

Prior to the establishment of the Kurdistan Workers' Party (PKK) in 1978, the story of Leyla Qasim served as inspiration to the women's struggle. Leyla started one of the first Kurdish Students Unions in Baghdad, and planned to hijack a plane to raise awareness of the Kurdish cause (comparisons can be drawn here to Leila Khaled, the Palestinian revolutionary whose act of political hijacking on behalf of the Popular Front for the Liberation of the Palestine helped to promote that national liberation struggle). She was caught before her plan could materialize and executed by the Iraqi state in 1974.

Kurdistan as a Colony, Women as the Oldest Colony

After the establishment of the PKK in the Turkish region of Kurdistan, the movement for Kurdish liberation was elevated to a higher level. The founders of the PKK, Abdullah Ocalan among them, deemed the creation of the organization necessary as the existing Turkish left had largely viewed the Kurdish question incorrectly, putting national chauvinism in command. This clashed with the thesis of the newly established party, which stated that Kurdistan was a colony, and that a national liberation struggle was a historical necessity.

Among the founders of the party was Sakine Cansiz, who would be murdered in Paris in 2013 alongside two other women leaders, Fidan Dogan and Leyla Sayleme. Sakine played a pivotal role in the development and growth of the organization, and a central role in the party's embrace of gender equality as a primary part of its makeup. Her leap into politics was itself an act of rebellion against the traditional family structure that aimed to keep her in bondage. Reflecting on her decision to become involved in political activities, she said, 'In a sense I abandoned the family. I did not accept that pressure, insisting on revolutionism. That's how I left and went to Ankara. In secret of course.'

The relationship of Sakine to Ocalan is important, as both were in leadership positions in the organization. It was the latter who through personal reflection and self-criticism of his own relationships with women began to question the patriarchal family structure in which women were always put in the position of being an object. He concluded that he needed to undergo a transformation by 'killing the man' inside himself, observing how society had made him the way he was. These reflections were in addition to looking back on other instances of women's oppression and subjugation he saw in his life, such as a childhood friend of his who was forcibly married to an old man, and seeing his mother live in what he saw as prison-like conditions within her own home. Most important to his decision to take up the issue of women's freedom on a higher level, though, was his relationship with Fatima, another founder of the party who he saw as someone he had used for his own interests.

Although Ocalan promoted the concept of 'killing the man' and advanced theoretical concepts relevant to women's liberation including that women constituted the oldest colony, he also understood that he – and men, in general – could not lead this process. He is viewed within the movement as someone who has given his strength and development to the process, but who has also actively encouraged women to take up leadership of their own liberation in an autonomous way within the party and other organizations in the wider movement.

Theoretical Basis of Jineologi

Today, the revolutionary movement that is grouped together in the Kurdistan Communities Group (KCK) in the four parts of Kurdistan advances the science of women, or Jineologi, as a principle theoretical and practical part of the revolutionary process. However, this concept, adopted in 2008, was the ideological culmination of decades of experience in organizing.

In addition to Ocalan's concept of 'killing the man', another fundamental idea is that of the 'theory of separation' (both put forward in 1996) which holds that women should be able to have control of their own organizations. If it is held that revolution cannot be made FOR the people, but rather by the people, then it must be held that revolution cannot merely be made FOR women, but must be made BY women. The separation theory also means that women should take themselves out of relationships that were based on hierarchies. One can see the seriousness today of this application, as romantic relationships and marriage within the ranks of cadre in the movement are non-existent. Part of this is to also protect the organizations from adopting a liberal approach to work and life.

Research into the role of women throughout the history of Mesopotamia also became a key part of the work of the movement towards the end of the 1990s. During the same year that Ocalan was captured in Kenya by the Turkish state, the PJKK was created as a women's party, although it was later superseded by other autonomous structures such as the PJA. In the 2000s, new theories were developed including the 'theory of the rose' which held that women may 'look fragile but have thorns to protect themselves'.

In the run-up to the new paradigm of democratic confederalism being adopted by the party and by the larger Kurdistan Communities Group (KCK) in 2005, a 'paradigm of a democratic, ecological society on the basis of women's freedom' was advocated in 2003.

For Self-Defence; Against Liberal Feminism and Orientalism

By the time the first day of my education about women's freedom in Kurdistan was half way over, I could understand why it was so important to begin with these classes rather than dive right into visiting organizations responsible for concrete, day-to-day issues and organizing. The instructors frequently spoke about how revolution isn't about taking power and then building something new, but struggling to overcome the ideology of capitalism *while* organizing, something that the movement had been doing for decades before Rojava came to prominence in 2012 with the establishment of the democratic self-administration.

Key to understanding Jineologi is that self-defence doesn't only mean taking up the gun, but actually manifests more frequently in building up structures and organization. As one leader in the movement told me with palpable revolutionary zeal, 'Self-defence also has to begin in the mind. If you see yourself as a victim, you can't overcome oppression.'

During the second day of education, there was an elaboration upon the history of feminist thought globally, including the first wave of the nineteenth and twentieth centuries, that focused on campaigns for the right to vote, equal civil rights and workers' rights, the second wave (1970-1990), which was characterized by slogans such as 'the private is political' and 'my body belongs to me', and the third wave since 1990 in which the deconstruction of genders has taken centre stage.

Importantly, and of critical interest to those in my class who had come from western societies, were reflections on how the state has attempted to liberalize the radical women's movement by funnelling money to various organizations, which has had the effect of bringing them within the framework of the capitalist system. In addition, the instructors spoke of the strand of liberal western feminism that often is orientalist in nature, and alluded to groups like FEMEN that equate Islam with women's oppression. Such groups promote the narrative of the imperialists who aim to subordinate the Middle East to their brand of capitalist modernity in the name of freedom. As one devoted Muslim woman who was also a dedicated part of the Rojava Revolution was to tell me a few days later of her hijab, 'It's not important what's on my head. It's important what's in my head.'

Key Components of Jineologi (The Science of Women)

The flexible and undogmatic approach of the Kurdish Freedom Movement to the idea of revolution and women's liberation was made clear to me during the instruction I received on what Jineologi means today as a science of women's liberation.

For instance, to the initial confusion and frustration of some of the internationalists, the instructors often didn't have cut and dry answers to give to certain questions. After all, Jineologi holds that there isn't some immutable one and only truth, but that the work done by revolutionaries in defence of humanity can give meaning to life and thus bring us closer to understanding the truth. However, they were clear about the fact that just because they don't see there as being 'one truth', this doesn't mean that one should lapse into the liberal approach of 'my truth' in which everyone's subjective analysis of reality has merit even if it's absurdly backward or reactionary.

Part of the analysis of Jineologi is to realize that everything and everyone is alive, and to not fall into the dichotomy of the material versus the immaterial. This may seem like quite a metaphysical approach for comrades in the west, who may be accustomed to much more materialist, and often positivist, approaches. The ideology also recognizes unity in diversity, understanding that advancements are made with solidarity and cooperation, but not through crushing individuality (as opposed to individualism).

Jineologi also recognizes the 'Principle of the Indefinite', which is that although the future cannot be predicted, humanity can analyze that there are different options and roads which can be taken and therefore we can intervene to change developments. Duality was spoken of often during instruction, and it was an idea that kept resurfacing during my visit to Rojava. As I was told about the war that continues to rage and the revolution that is unfolding at the same time: 'By seeing that there's light, we become aware of the darkness. One cannot exist without the other. There are contradicting parts.'

Other aspects to the ideology included not separating subject and object, as well as creating unity between emotional and analytical intelligence. As the instructor made clear, 'On the one hand, we criticize rationalism. Emotional intelligence played a key role in the Neolithic period. We can be both. We can both think and feel.'

Five Principles of Women's Liberation Ideology

These concepts help to illustrate the major theoretical work that has gone into creating this science of women, but the actual principles of the ideology can be underlined as the following:

1. Welatparezi
   To reject estrangement, colonialism, assimilation imposed on women
2. Free Thought / Opinion
   Women must make their own decisions and make a mental break with the structures that dominate

3. Autonomous Women's Organizing
   Only if women have the chance to organize themselves will patriarchy be overcome
4. Struggle for Change
   Not merely making demands of the oppressor, but taking rights through struggle and creating alternatives
5. Aesthetic and Ethics
   Women should not stick to patterns of beauty dictated by society or men

From Theory to Practice

Of course, theory without any kind of practical application is meaningless, and the Kurdish Freedom Movement has gone through a process of constantly refining and developing its theories related to emancipating half of the human race.

Even within the movement itself, there have been no lack of incidents – including involving leadership – that have shown that revolutionary organizations themselves are not immune from patriarchal attitudes.

For instance, in the beginning of women participating in the armed struggle in Bakur, many men within the PKK had an attitude that women were incapable of taking on certain tasks that were deemed to be 'manly'. The argument from some men in leadership was that women were too emotional and soft for warfare, and that therefore it was better to place them in non-guerrilla roles. Some commanders wanted their women comrades who did become guerrillas to wear scarves.

One young woman fighter, Heval Beritan, heard about this and suggested that women build up their own guerrilla forces. The autonomous organization and separation of the men from the women guerrillas that followed had the effect of meaning that men and women had to take care of all tasks now (for instance, men were now completely responsible for cooking).

The story of Heval Beritan is one that clearly illustrates

the fact that women are at the very least on par with men in terms of being able to accomplish every revolutionary task and play every role. She was initially a journalist, but wound up a commander in warfare as she wanted to play a more hands-on role in the struggle. In 1992 during the South War, she fought until her last bullet and rather than submit to being captured by the reactionary forces of the KDP, threw herself from a mountain, committing revolutionary suicide in the same vein as Bese had done so more than 50 years before during the battle of Dersim.

The lives of the Beritans, the Sakines and the other countless women revolutionaries in Kurdistan provided the practical example for the women who went on to form the YPJ.

Today's women's revolution in Rojava would have been an impossible dream without the examples of these shehids (martyrs) who gave their lives for the cause of not only freedom for Kurds, but for women everywhere. Every day, the soil of Rojava is given life by the blood of women who fall in combat, side by side with their male comrades as equals. The self-sacrifice of those like Arin Markin, who blew herself up during the battle of Kobane rather than be taken prisoner by Daesh, illuminates the path of women, as does YPJ/SDF Commander Rojda Felat who was at the forefront of the Raqqa operation. Their examples are the practical manifestation of the ideology developed over decades of struggle, one that the movement believes has the potential to not only liberate the Middle East, but the whole of humankind.

Chapter 6

The Centrality of Women's Liberation in Northern Syria (Practice)

The scene couldn't be more jubilant. The sun shines brightly in a way that is simultaneously agonizing and unbearable, yet beautifully brilliant. Scores of packed cars and Toyota trucks with men and women clutching tri-colour Rojavan flags make their way to a makeshift parking lot in the middle of what appears to be a seemingly endless field. The colours are vibrant and festive, indicative of the Kurdish nation's cultural traditions and identity. Smiles abound as thousands descend on a massive public gathering, one that everyone knew was going to take place on this day, even though the location had only been announced the previous night. Security is tight. After all, this is still a warzone despite the liberatory feeling that reigns supreme.

Over what is otherwise picture-perfect scenery in Dirbesiye, the newly constructed Turkish border wall isn't far off. On that side of the divide that keeps this nation torn apart, Kurds are subject to the brutality of a colonial state they have been fighting for what seems like an eternity.

Women too, Kurdish or Turkish alike, are subject to the demeaning policies of Recep Tayyip Erdogan's AKP Party, an organization that proposed just last year that rapists should be pardoned if they marry their victims. Erdogan himself has proclaimed that women are not equal to men in blunt, and unmistakable terms.

Standing on this piece of free territory over the barely completed border wall, life couldn't be more different. Today is 8 March, or International Women's Day. It's a day that is easily one of the most important in the calendar in northern Syria, along with Newroz and perhaps 15 March, the day that

Abdullah Ocalan was captured in 1999.

Driving through Cizire canton to get to the festival, banners lined the roads proclaiming 'Adure 8' as a day to be celebrated. Walls brightened up the city of Amude, painted with the most stunning murals marking the importance of this day. Women hold up half the sky, the old Chinese saying goes. Here, the desire for the slogan to be more than just words is palpable. It's not just that women have been given guns to defend their lives and their newly claimed freedom, although that's without a doubt an important component of it, perhaps the most visual representation of all of the work taking place within the society to raise women up to genuine equality.

Women's autonomous organizations were among the first to be set up here, even before the revolution was announced in 2012. It's groups such as Kongreya Star that have entrusted themselves with the responsibility of putting together this festive display of celebration and struggle.

As I walk through the field filled with thousands of people from all ethnic backgrounds and age groups, that spirit of revolution I've alluded to before grabs me and takes full hold of me. I'm startled by the juxtaposition of the stage in front of me, behind which a banner of Serok Apo (Abdullah Ocalan) hangs proudly, and the border wall that I can make out maybe a few hundred metres behind it. The Turkish forces have hung a flag of the increasingly fascist Republic over it, as if the disgusting slabs of concrete weren't enough to cement the idea that the occupiers were always watching. And yet, Rojava's self-defence forces are ever vigilant and ready to do battle.

A young man I've just met from one of the Turkish communist parties that has sent militants to fight in Rojava puts his arm over me and tells me, 'On that side of the border today, women will be beaten and arrested for demonstrating. No matter if they're in Istanbul, Ankara or Cizire. Same shit.'

Here, though, women dance. Women sing. Women shout.

Women demand their emancipation. As part of moving from object to subject, from oppressed to equals, women are in motion. They are the backbone of this revolution.

Kongreya Star

The day before attending the International Women's Day festivities, I was fortunate enough to be able to visit the head office of Kongreya Star in Qamishlo, the capital city of both Cizire canton and the federation.

As the women here are eager to tell me, the position of the women's movement in Rojava today wouldn't be even close to where it is if it wasn't for the work the movement had done over decades prior to 2012 in all four parts of Kurdistan. Here, the first independent women's organization, Yekitiya Star, had been founded in 2005, but they faced immense challenges in organizing freely due to opposition and restrictions from the Syrian state. This was the forerunner to the current organization that adopted its new name to reflect the entirety of the federation.

As three women hevals are keen to tell me, theirs is a structure that aims to tackle hierarchy, and therefore organizes from the base. As the commune is the basis for the new society being set up in Rojava, it is within that structure that problems concerning women are first addressed (each commune has a representative of Kongreya Star within it). If, however, they cannot be handled within the commune, they then go to their regional Kongreya Star group. If the problem requires an even higher level of mediation or assistance, central Kongreya Star is then consulted. The aim of the organization as a whole is to tackle every problem that concerns the lives of women today in northern Syria, which is no small task given the backwardness that women have had to confront and attempt to overcome.

Undoing Patriarchal Mentalities in Men

One of the most difficult aspects of organizing has been

the resistance to the notion of women's empowerment that comes from men who are still rooted in traditional patriarchal mentalities.

As one of the younger hevals explains to me, this is changing gradually, and a noticeable difference is already apparent in 5 years of organizing. She explains to me how even though the entirety of the Kurdish nation has been oppressed, men have had the power over women in the home.

'Men often don't want women working in politics, or outside of the home in general. There is a fear of them leaving their so-called mother role.'

It should come as no surprise that women receive education here about the history of the Kurdish women's movement and the theoretical basis for women's liberation in Kurdish society known as Jineologi. What I found more surprising – and deeply impressive – are the lengths to which the organization is also going to educate men.

I'm told that in the city of Afrin, there was just recently an educational strictly for men that focused on 5,000 years of male hegemony. There are classes across the whole of the region that last for weeks, or even months for those serious about 'killing the dominant male' inside themselves. These aim to do more than just educate – they are akin to a form of rehabilitation to overcome reactionary attitudes towards gender roles and patriarchal oppression. The courses are given by both women and men, and aim to cut out attitudes ranging from extremely overt sexism to the more subtle but still sexist attitudes of, 'I need to protect her because I don't want to see her hurt' (assuming the position of men is to protect women because of the superior role of men and asserting that women cannot defend or protect themselves).

The youngest of the hevals continues, 'Male chauvinism is obvious even in those who talk about women's liberation. They might be able to speak on it theoretically, but often can't really back it up in practice.'

I find her words extremely relevant on a personal level. How many of us men in the west who would call ourselves feminists, even those of us who have histories of many years in socialist and radical political life, fall short on questions of practice on this very issue? My experience has been that more than any other question, it is relations between men and women in which male 'comrades' often fall far short of the mark. To be sure, this cannot ultimately be rectified without revolution, and without a doubt the omnipresence of extreme sexism in our uber-capitalist societies can't help but taint even the most serious of male revolutionaries with a level of reactionary characteristics.

Yet, it seems to me that the model employed here by Kongreya Star in how serious re-education for men is taken might be something that radicals in the west should consider beyond just simple theoretical pronouncements about equality.

Making Women's Empowerment Permanent

Although the idea of bringing men into the work being done by Kongreya Star is an important component, men do not participate in any way in the organization's structure. Just as the Women's Protection Units (YPJ) is an autonomous force fighting alongside the YPG that has its own structure of leadership, Kongreya Star makes decisions on its own without the input of men.

As I'm told many times in Rojava, there are two struggles unfolding at the moment – a military one against Daesh, and a women's struggle in all aspects of society. For the women's struggle to be successful, it is up to women themselves to achieve and defend their free life.

Of course, there are concerns among the women of Kongreya Star here about the long-term vitality of the movement.

As Heval Amuda says, 'In many previous revolutions, women would play a very central role including in fighting. But at the end of the day, they would go home, back to their previous positions in the traditional family. We want to make sure that doesn't happen here. Sometimes a woman can think more like a man than a man himself.'

The women here have all experienced the transformation of liberation that has taken place both inside of themselves and in the greater fabric of society. As they don't hesitate to point out, in the beginning many of them didn't believe themselves (and these are now leaders!) that women could do everything that men could. It was a process that meant eroding the uncertainty of being able to be equal slowly but surely, while building the self-confidence needed to assert themselves.

They are quick to point out that their freedom is not the western, liberal conception of what it means to be liberated in which, 'I can go, do and speak what I want', but it is inextricably linked up with the collective liberation of the entirety of the people. They are blunt about their objection to the former concept in asserting that this westernized notion 'isn't freedom at all'. Theirs is a fight that is ideological, philosophical and, above all, practical – one that takes stock of the historic role of the entirety of the revolutionary movement.

The Work of Mala Jin

A short walk from the central organization of Kongreya Star is the local Mala Jin, or 'house for women'. This project was initially started by just four women, but today there are thousands who work in a number of these houses all across northern Syria. Their work focuses on giving women a place to come if they need help or strength, particularly in the fight against domestic violence and abuse.

As I'm told, prior to 2011 the levels of domestic violence were high as this was a time before widespread education about the rights of women that the democratic self-administration ushered in. With the coming of the revolution in 2012, a process began that saw the domestic abuse numbers fall, though there was initially a considerable amount of threats by men against the house and its leadership because of the work they were involved in. These threats haven't completely been done away with yet, but I'm told the situation is vastly improved. Also, as a testament to the transformation of family relations, most of the women who come to Mala Jin today are not coming from abusive households, but are Arab women who were previously in the hands of Daesh.

At this particular house, there are 11 women who volunteer their time to assist with the work. As is the case everywhere in Rojava, everything is built from the bottom up. It is families and individuals who have donated not just their time, but their money and resources to help in building this and other houses across northern Syria.

I'm stunned to hear just how hands-on Mala Jin truly is in insuring the liberation of their sisters, going as far as to go to homes with force to physically liberate women who are confined by their husbands.

Yet, even when men initially appear beyond the point of rehabilitation, there is always an attempt made at resolution. If a woman is taken to freedom, or she escapes from home by herself, there will usually follow a collective sit down with the man and the family. If these efforts of resolving the situation aren't successful, the man can then be taken to the Asayish (security service), but this is generally a last resort. Even then, a simple punishment is not the norm for men who have been engaged in domestic abuse, but restorative justice that attempts to actually change the man's thinking and behaviour is applied. In all cases, women and their children can be taken to houses where they can live in safety and security if they are under threat of physical or emotional harm.

With the coming of self-administration, a gap was left in terms of the law. As I was to find out, many changes have taken place in this sphere as it applies to the role of women. One example has been the outlawing of forced marriages. While common prior to

2012, now families responsible can be fined, or even imprisoned if absolutely necessary. In an effort to overcome polygamy, all religious marriages (nikkahs) must now be done together with a legal marriage to make sure that a man cannot marry more than one woman. I'm also told that while marriage between relatives wasn't unusual just half a decade ago, such occurrences today are few and far between.

Fear of Freedom?

As I stand in the middle of such tremendous natural beauty the next day in Dirbesiye, I couldn't think of a more ideal place to be spending International Women's Day.

Speakers take the stage to chants of 'Jin Jiyan Azadi' (Woman, Life, Freedom). Performers sing songs in Kurdish with the passion and urgency of a people who have kept their national customs under wraps – but always still in their spirits – for decades. Young children born after the start of the revolution carelessly play in the fields. Are they oblivious to the major historical earthquake that's taking place here, one that they are part of whether they know it yet or not?

I ask a young woman comrade I've just met from the Turkish-based Marxist-Leninist Communist Party (MLKP) if she's encountered a fear from women in Rojavan society about grabbing hold of their own freedom. She seems perplexed, but I explain that I'm asking because of something that was said the day before at the Mala Jin. One of the women there had said that women are often fearful about coming to the house, but once they arrive, they're often so moved by their experience that they end up not only breaking free from their household shackles, but also join the revolution in some organizational capacity. The MLKP heval nods an approving 'I understand' then cuts me off quickly saying, 'That's true for all of us. I also had to overcome that traditionalist family environment and the subjugation that comes with it. But once you take that first step, the leap to being a revolutionary doesn't seem that big after all. My family wanted to have me married off, but I became a guerrilla for the people.'

It seems that this 'leap' is precisely what the whole of society here has taken. The fear and uncertainty of self-administration, the doubts about women taking the reins of leadership, certainly had to exist at some point.

However, just as so many individual women now walk chin up with an unbreakable confidence, the whole of Rojava appears as such to me. Even with Turkish soldiers positioned not far off with tanks and heavy weaponry, a confidence of victory pervades this strip of liberated land and its people armed with 40-year-old Kalashnikovs and ideas that belong to the future of humankind.

My newest heval has to abruptly leave, so we exchange the customary handshake and 'Serkeftin' (victory). She leaves me with one last message, a slogan that is plastered on a number of buildings and banners across Cizire canton: 'If not now, when? If not us, who?'

It's evident that for these women, there is no going back. Fear seems to have been vanquished. It seems contradictory for me to say so of a society that makes every statement it can to confirm its anti-hierarchical and anti-vanguard sentiments, but these women *are* the leadership – not merely of northern Syria, but, I would argue, the world. I am free of any level of doubt that they are in fact the vanguard force of humanity.

Chapter 7

Rojavan Pedagogy: Where Students Are Also Teachers

Revolutionary culture is often thought of as the forging of something completely new in the process of radically transforming society. The old ideas of the establishment are thrown into the dustbin of history and replaced wholesale with ones that represent the formerly subjugated and downtrodden.

Of course, it's never been quite as easy or cut and dry as this in the practice of any revolution to date. Also, in societies that have seen indigenous cultures repressed by the powers that be, those marginalized and sometimes illegal forms of expression can by the virtue of their very antagonism with the state be revolutionary in character despite not being in any meaningful sense 'new'.

Such is the reality today in northern Syria, in which not only the Kurdish language and culture, but also those of the between 25 or 30 ethnic groups other than Arabs who reside there, are once again being analyzed and practised.

Nonetheless, the reality is that a 'return to the old' is full of immense contradictions. The Kurdish Freedom Movement often speaks of a 'return to the natural society', but this isn't meant in a rigid fashion. If all elements of the colonized culture are practised mechanically, this isn't at all the same as bringing into being a revolutionary culture. It isn't enough to the radicals in Rojava that 'Kurdish culture' in some abstract sense is reclaimed. The question becomes, what *kind* of Kurdish culture? There is indeed a profound difference between the culture of narrow and traditional nationalism that is the officialdom of the education system in Iraq's Kurdistan Region, and those of the internationalists who are the vanguard of change in northern

Syria, for instance. It's possible that elements of the reclaimed culture, especially if they represent feudal ideas, are reactionary and need to be replaced with something that makes a radical break from that past.

My background as a hip-hop artist from the west whose music contains a progressive, socialist message provoked serious interest in the way that the arts are being practised today in Rojava 5 years after the so-called democratic self-administration took over the reins of organizing society from the Syrian Arab state. I was fascinated to see what had become of the old schools that had only taught in the Arabic language, and beyond that only taught Arab culture in what is such an ethnically diverse region.

Entering the Shehid Yekta Herekol Academy

Situated just 30 kilometres east of Qamishlo, the de-facto capital of the DFSNS, is the town of Tirbespiye. It may not be easy to find on a map by its Kurdish name today, as its official name within the Syrian Arab Republic is still al-Qahtaniyah.

Arriving in the town of about 16,000 residents, the group of internationalists that I'm travelling with first pulls up to a checkpoint of the Asayish. After being waved through, I can see a group of maybe a dozen teenagers preparing to greet our caravan at the front entrance of what is one of the region's first revolutionary academies for the practice of the arts. As I step foot onto the sidewalk and walk up to the gates of the institution, a young man of not more than 18 reaches for my hand and says in English 'Welcome to the Shehid Yekta Herekol Academy'.

The institution's name, like so many others in northern Syria today, pays homage to a martyr of the Kurdish Freedom Movement. Yekta Herekol, born in Dersim in 1968, studied theatre in Ankara until the early 1990s when he was confronted with the discriminatory practices of the Turkish state towards his native culture. After deciding to join the PKK in the mountains, he was caught on two occasions by the Turkish authorities but managed to eventually travel abroad where he developed his artistic capabilities further. However, while free to practise his culture openly in Greece and Russia, he yearned for his home soil, and decided to return to Kurdistan. In 2003, he entered Rojava and joined demonstrations in Qamishlo on 12 March 2004. Two weeks later in Halab (Aleppo), he burned himself to death in a sign of protest, not only against the central government's repression of Kurdish expression, but as a critique of the movement to 'do its work properly and reinforce the struggle'.

Walking into the main hall of the academy, it felt like I had entered into a museum of the future. There were beautiful paintings and sculptures to be seen everywhere, ones that made me question if it was possible that people as young as those I had just met could really be responsible for such wondrous creations. As it turns out, all of the work that was to be seen here was the achievement of these incredibly talented students. Our group received a tour of the two floors of the academy, with room after room full of tools for the practise of the arts – costumes for theatre performances, musical instruments, brushes and easels for painting. In the courtyard, there was a green space that the students and the teachers plan on converting into a full garden in the near future. We were then led into the kitchen where a small group of students were preparing lunch, before being summoned to what seemed like an impromptu musical performance by another group of youths.

Hevalti (Comradeship) Between Student and Teacher

It feels strange using the expressions 'student' or 'teacher' to refer to the roles of those who are receiving education at the academy and those who are responsible for instruction.

Actually, the distinction is much more blurred than at institutions in capitalist societies, or perhaps even in some socialist ones. I very quickly realized that the relationship between students and teachers here doesn't take on the kind of characteristics of subordination that I had grown up with. I recall going to school, being told what to think (as opposed to methods of how to think), cramming information into my brain, making sure I didn't challenge my teachers too much and taking exams that I felt were rather worthless the bulk of the time. Retaining information over the long-haul was barely even a thought.

Here in Rojava, I encountered something radically different, a type of learning paradigm that reminded me of the ideas put forward in Paolo Freire's *Pedagogy of the Oppressed*. As I was told by one of the students, a 17-year-old by the name of Gelhat, 'We're all students and teachers. That's the way we are organized and how we have found that we learn best.'

That's not to say there's no official structure, of course. The academy has a Reverberi, roughly translated as leadership, but it isn't an administration that is untouchable or unaccountable to those who are enrolled there. (As in all administrations in Rojava, 50 per cent of the Reverberi must be women).

There didn't seem to be the kind of intimidating presence here on behalf of the leadership that I remember so well in my schools. As I'm told by one of these 'administrators':

> we have a weekly tekmil (a criticism and self-criticism session) in which the students and us reflect together on what we are critical about in ourselves, what we could have done more effectively, and what suggestions we have moving forward. Also, this is where students can make criticisms of the Reverberi. Our relationship is based on the concept of hevalti (comradeship). It is not hierarchical.

To the foreign ear, these were shocking concepts on the one hand, but on the other they seemed to echo common sense. What better way to really get at the root of how to enhance a learning experience than to have a forum for how to make it more productive rather than repressing suggestions for improvement? This seemed to be a truly radical concept when coming out of the halls of 'learning' in the west. It seemed profoundly revolutionary to think that the teachers could be criticized in such a direct fashion and not take it personally, or to not respond by 'disciplining' the students. To break down the barrier of separation and the 'untouchable' teacher who was there to inorganically implant knowledge into the student was something I had long dreamt of, and here I was seeing it in action. I realized then, though, that it wasn't just my foreign ears that this must have seemed strange to – at one point, these students must have felt exactly the same way.

I was deeply curious about just how much the education in this region of the country has transformed since the self-administration took control in 2012.

As one of the members of the Reverberi tells me:

This academy itself used to be a cultural centre of the state. But at that time, it was inconceivable that young people from the background of these students who are here today would have access to it. It was for the elites, and primarily for Arabs. We are now trying to build up the democratic nation, so our goal is to have students from all kinds of backgrounds, not just Kurds. Of course, because of the repression of the Kurdish culture, this has so far been our focus, as the students already know Arab culture very well from their previous instruction before the revolution.

Adding to the words of this instructor was a young woman of 17, who spoke of just how different the learning environment was now as opposed to before 2012. 'I remember at that time if a student was seen as not learning the official curriculum adequately, we would be beaten. Now we are teaching classes. It's like night and day.'

Structure of the Academy

The teaching she was referring to is the fact that once a month, each student is responsible for creating a lesson and facilitating it for the rest of the class.

At this academy, opened only in the fall of 2015, there are currently 35 students, as well as four from the previous term that have stayed on in a supportive role. Unlike the institutions I have been used to my entire life, the term of learning here isn't for several years, but rather 15 months. This isn't necessarily considered the ideal length of time that students should spend at the academy, but as I'm told 'it's sped up because of the war. We have urgent needs in society in general, so once students truly master their disciplines, they're of course needed elsewhere to contribute their skills.'

The youngest of these students is 13, and the oldest are around 20. Unlike our western high schools or secondary schools, there is no grade or year distinction. The 13-year-olds sit in the same lessons as their fellow students who are up to 7 years older than they are. During the present term, there are five music teachers, four teaching cinema and four for dance. Daily education consists of 4 hours of instruction in the morning and 3 in the afternoon, 5 days a week. This amounts to a total of 35 hours of instruction per week.

It's telling that the day-to-day running of the academy is not only done by the students, but democratically planned by them in a collective fashion. In addition to the kitchen work, the logistics and cleaning of the centre are all done in a communal fashion. This is a centre in which the students not only learn during the day, but also sleep, so they are all entrusted with the responsibility of taking care of their learning and living environment.

Academies Rather Than Universities

The idea of the free academy (there are of course no tuition fees here) was a suggestion of Kurdish Freedom Movement leader Abdullah Ocalan, who saw their establishment as a way of replacing the existing state university structure.

As I'm told, there are similarities to traditional universities or schools in the sense that there are some examinations, but the difference is that if the student doesn't succeed the first time around, they aren't told they have failed or kicked out of the academy. In addition, although diplomas or certificates are issued, the primary focus is on really mastering subjects and disciplines rather than just having a piece of paper to prove that the academy was attended and using that to then gain 'success' in society by being able to earn more money than if one hadn't attended the academy. As one student told me, 'Maybe to you it looks on the surface like a university, but the content is radically different.'

Perhaps in the context of our societies, we often think of art as being created simply for the purpose of the art itself. This isn't necessarily true, as all art has an ideological orientation (including when art claims to be above ideology or non-ideological).

At this academy, there is an emphasis on the historical, philosophical, aesthetical, ideological, political and social sides of art and culture. There are currently 30 areas of study, which all aim to contribute to the motto put forward by the Reverberi: 'We want to create an artist who is able to take off the mask of those in power; an artist who is creating the basis for destroying their power. This institution is taking our voice and our feelings back from our enemy and giving voice to all other peoples oppressed by the occupying system.'

Confronting Problems and Contradictions

As with every institution in Rojava, there are no lack of problems that confront the development of them. After all, how else could it be in a war situation? This revolution isn't unfolding under ideal conditions, but in the midst of a scenario in which the literal survival of the population isn't a foregone conclusion. Still, there is an atmosphere of humour and light-heartedness that is able to pervade the environment at the academy.

When I ask one of the Reverberi what the main problem is confronting the academy, he says perhaps half jokingly, 'You know the youth: they don't want to sit in class, but run around and be playful all the time!' I glance over at one of the students, who lets off a mischievous smile in my direction, the kind that my friends and I used to make when we were up to no good in class. Even here, in a cooperative and democratic learning environment, the youthful spirit of rebellion was inescapable.

Becoming more serious, the comrade from the Reverberi tells me, 'Each student brings with them the influence of the occupying system, as well as the influence of the traditional Kurdish society. Our goal is to transform these ideologies. Ten per cent of our fight is against an external enemy and ninety per cent is internal.'

He also makes a fascinating point about the kind of discipline needed to overcome socialization from the old society. 'When you tell these young people to go fight in the YPG, they are all for it, but when you say sit down and read, they say no. Study requires immense effort, perhaps much more effort than fighting.'

In addition to the problems of youth that were alluded to, it was pointed out that the culture of traditionalism still prevalent in society has prevented some students who have wanted to attend the academy from being able to due to their families. This underscores the importance of the work of the centre, as what happens inside the halls of learning has a dialectical relationship with what takes place in the larger society, including the views held by mothers and fathers. It is hoped that in due time, attitudes among the older generation that prevent their sons and daughters from coming to such places of learning to live and study will gradually be eroded.

That gradual, yet very real, transformation of human beings was on full display in the students that I met. It was clear that they were developing revolutionary ethics and personalities. The academy is already sending some of its students to cities such as Derik, Qamishlo and Kobane for periods of 2 months with the task of educating ten people in the arts. They are entrusted with responsibility that our youth in the west wouldn't dare to be given by administrators in any centre of learning.

Dancing into the Future

I confess that I've never quite been as embarrassed as I was the evening after the seminar that my internationalist group received on the history of the academy and the structure of learning being developed in Rojava had finished. We were going to spend the night at the academy with the students, and activities that transcend the language barrier are always the best ways of getting to know people on some level. The embarrassment had already begun hours earlier during a break in the programme, when my 'internationalist' team had suffered what must have been among history's worst volleyball losses. In fairness to us, the students of the academy probably practise on an almost daily basis since they have a net right in front of the school's entrance, so miracles could not have been expected.

However, I was later crying out for some sort of divine intervention when they dragged us onto the dancefloor that night to partake in traditional Kurdish dance. Unfortunately, there was no place to hide from either the eyes or the cameras of the students. They had a pretty hearty laugh at our expense – well, perhaps not *at* our expense, as we laughed off the embarrassment maybe even harder than they did.

As the amusement from the evening's hours of bonding had started to wind down, we all came back to reality when we realized how late it was. By 10 pm, generally the students are in their rooms preparing to rest, but it was nearly 11 and we were still drenched in sweat from hours of dancing (I use that word loosely in my case).

Situated across the road from the main hall is where some of the male students live, in a setting comparable to a western university's dormitories. We walked out into the brisk evening air and crossed the road. I couldn't help but think back to my college experience about 15 years earlier. I remember the countless times that I would head back to my dorm room after the seemingly never-ending college parties, usually drunk and stumbling. Truth be told, I didn't have much respect for my college experience because frankly I felt as if the institution didn't have a great deal of respect for me. I couldn't relate to the experience in which I felt like I wasn't learning a great deal, never felt challenged and where teachers acted as if they were generally untouchable. It didn't speak to me whatsoever. The only real part of college that I truly enjoyed – and I guarantee this is the case for a huge amount of college and university students from the US – were those parties on Friday and Saturday nights which were a reprieve from the boring, rigid instruction received during the week. The alienation I felt of being in school turned later to the alienation of the workforce. The only solace of mine was to be found in going out on a Friday night and in forgetting about the existence of my exploitation.

Yet, here I was in the middle of the Syrian war, and I found something remarkably different. I wished I could be the age of these students again so that I could attend a centre of learning like the one I had just set foot in. There wouldn't be the inclination to 'get drunk' or to try to find other exciting escapes from the mundane and stifling confines of the western university. Here was a pedagogy in development that respected the student as a master of his or her destiny, as a part of a greater whole and a movement towards human liberation. The example of what I had witnessed was powerful.

Though in the west I count myself as fortunate to be able to sleep peacefully each night with no worries about the approach of fascist forces on my doorstep, I simultaneously feel envious that the youth of Rojava have the luxury of getting to construct a brand new educational and cultural system. It's a luxury that of course isn't very luxurious at all, as the self-defence forces are paying for the defence of these students in blood each and every day. To quote Lincoln Steffens after he visited the Soviet Union in the early years of the revolution, 'I have seen the future and it works.' This time, however, let's hope that the future is written more beautifully and victoriously.

Chapter 8

The Theory, Practice and Contradictions of Internationalism in Rojava

The first week of my month-long visit to Rojava was reserved for theoretical and ideological education. After initially receiving a full day of instruction on the history of the Kurdish Freedom Movement, the comrades announced that the following day the group of internationalist activists I had come to northern Syria with would be sitting through another all-day session.

As someone who had been eager to travel to this profoundly revolutionary society for what seemed like an eternity, who had absorbed thousands of pages of books and articles, and watched everything I could get my hands on about Rojava, my initial reaction was disappointment. After all, couldn't I have had all this education and done all this theoretical preparation back at home in Europe? In fact, hadn't I already done a great deal of this political study on my own? I was perhaps quite understandably impatient to get out and see the unfolding social revolution for myself, and to participate in it through my journalistic work, especially considering that this trip to the heartland of this century's most profound anti-fascist struggle had been years in the making.

However, when I now look back on the education that I received during that first week which laid the ground for the rest of the month I spent there, I'm full of appreciation for how important it was and why it was deemed a necessary part of my immersion in a new society.

After all, as our Kurdish comrades pointed out, this was not to be a delegation of diplomats, and we shouldn't approach Rojava through the eyes of a mere visitor, or spectator. Concern was also paid to the prospect of the trip appearing to be nothing more than an expression of 'revolutionary tourism' (I still have those concerns, and I'm not sure that there's necessarily a way to prevent that from at least partially being true).

I now fully realize that to be active as part of the revolution, to be inside of it as a participant and not merely an observer, receiving at least a basic overview of the theory that illuminates the path of the revolution from those directly involved in pushing this process forward is vital.

Anarchists and Communists United Against Dogma

Our delegation's second educational session was to focus on the concept of internationalism, which was no doubt of heightened relevance considering the foreign makeup of the group I was with (within that group of multiple nationalities, we had Germans, Italians, Spaniards, Catalonians and Swiss nationals).

I was relieved that I wasn't the only comrade in the group who had such a low-level – in fact, in all truthfulness practically non-existent – understanding of the Kurdish language. Unfortunately, because we all spoke so many different languages, it turned out that by the end of the month, my Kurdish wasn't all that vastly improved, but my understanding of a few other languages was, mainly German owing to the substantial number of internationalists who had joined this trip from there. This was characteristic of the decades-long solidarity that has existed between the PKK and elements of the German left.

When I had first met this group of progressive-minded activists while en route from Europe to northern Iraq, my first wonder was what their political backgrounds were. After all, I had assumed due to what some have termed the 'ideological eclecticness' of the Rojava project that in order to travel there, a leftist cannot be of the dogmatic strand. To be rigid in one's thinking is anathema to the social regeneration that's taking place in northern Syria. It is a revolution that frustrates those activists who find that elements of it can't neatly fit into their preconceptions of what such a process should look like, or their puritanical visions that lose their value as soon as they depart from the comfort of their coffee shop militancy. Their neatly defined boxes can't be ticked by the contradiction-laden process, so it's better in their eyes that they either reject it as ultra-leftist, opportunist, pro-imperialist, on the one hand; or to simply ignore it or underestimate its importance for twenty-first century revolution and for humanity. This is deeply ego driven, and reflects the political culture of far too much of the western leftist tendency to overinflate the importance of their micro-sects.

As it turned out, the majority of the activists who I was with had backgrounds in various anarchist and 'libertarian socialist' movements in Europe. This didn't surprise me, as over the past 5 years, the Kurdish resistance in northern Syria has been far more discussed in those circles than in revolutionary Marxist ones. After all, the Kurdistan Communities Group (KCK), of which the Rojava's Democratic Union Party (PYD) is a member, adheres to the non-state ideology of democratic confederalism adopted by Abdullah Ocalan and the Kurdistan Workers' Party (PKK) in the mid-2000s after the international plot that has left him in solitary confinement on the Imrali Island from 1999 to this day.

Despite this 'libertarian' ideological turn, elements of the Turkish-based communist movement (who do not have social chauvinist politics that relegate or trample on the Kurdish question), have also been supportive of Rojava's process. Most notably, the Marxist-Leninist Communist Party (MLKP) set up the International Freedom Battalion (IFB) in 2014, which aimed to rekindle the spirit of the International Brigades that fought on behalf of the Spanish Republic against the fascism of Franco in the 1930s. Communist volunteers have fought side by side with anarchist volunteers within and outside the IFB as part of the YPG and YPJ.

This undogmatic leftist characteristic of the revolution makes it truly unique on the world stage at this juncture in history – usually in western societies, socialist groups have enough trouble as it is joining hands in coalition-related work with those with very similar, if not identical politics, let alone those who hold drastically different views on the role of the state. This revolution seems to show that something dramatically different is possible, and I'm convinced it goes beyond merely the military aspect of the struggle.

This isn't to say, however, that this means that Rojava is a place that internationalists arrive in and suddenly our ideological differences vanish, or are glossed over. In fact, the opposite is true in many ways.

I have to confess that as somebody with a revolutionary Marxist background, I didn't always feel comfortable at the beginning of the trip when learning about the political orientations of my new comrades. Are these *really* my comrades? I battled internally throughout the first few days, aiming to convince myself that in fact what I was going through was part of a detox of the sectarian mindset. It's not that I was going to concede that my views on key ideological matters or on political organization were somehow wrong. If I could be proved wrong, that's one thing – and I had to open myself up to at least the possibility of that.

After all, the point of my trip wasn't to simply look for evidence that proved my theories correct. I had to remind myself that this experience was about understanding how the new paradigm adopted by the Kurdish Freedom Movement came to fruition because of deep, self-critical reflection of socialism in the twentieth century, and the successes and failures of the Kurdish organizational model itself. If the movement could do that and emerge successful on a new level in the twenty-first century at a time when generally the world revolution had been ebbing, then I needed to carry with me the same self-critical and open spirit.

The debates began early into our travel, almost as soon as

we had touched the ground in Mesopotamia. On the second night that we were all together, we decided to get to know each other in a somewhat formal manner – call it the good old 'going around the room, letting everyone know our names and a bit about each other' technique.

I was a bit apprehensive on this occasion, despite the fact that shyness is seldom a trait one could accuse me of possessing. I didn't know how much information I should divulge about my political history or my worldview. I was scared of being judged or misunderstood (especially with so many languages being spoken). I don't remember exactly what I said, but it must have come out as a bit ambiguous, because when the entire group had taken their turns and we were all set to break out into different activities for the rest of the night, one of the comrades said, 'You know, I was so worried that the men on this trip were all going to be these Marxist-Leninist types.'

Hold up – now here's something I couldn't let fly! I didn't let anyone else even begin to attempt to reply at that moment, replying quite firmly, 'Maybe I wasn't clear, but my politics are of the revolutionary Marxist type that you speak of.' That's all it took for the wishy-washy and liberal unity that had so far prevailed to be broken. The polemics kicked off. We talked about the role of Marx, who some viewed as racist and thus they believed that many of his economic ideas should be discredited, the experiences of 'actually existing socialism', and a multitude of other subjects.

These debates happened throughout that evening and night, for the next week and for the next month. They were largely, although frankly not always entirely, conducted in a spirit of comradeship that was pleasantly surprising, mostly because in the west I have yet to see a debate of this kind not only last an appropriate amount of time, but because usually it devolves quite quickly into people's feelings getting hurt or taking arguments personally. In that geography and under these circumstances, however, here were undogmatic communists and anarchists having these pivotal conversations in a way that contributed to a feeling of mutual respect and ideological growth.

Examples of Internationalism in the Nineteenth and Twentieth Centuries

During the day-long education session on the relevance of internationalism in the Kurdish Freedom Movement, the hevals who facilitated the instruction paid attention to five particular periods and struggles in the nineteenth and twentieth centuries they deemed to be important.

The first was the creation of the internationals that aimed to group the revolutionary movement together, beginning with the International Workers' Association, or First International, started at the initiative of Karl Marx in 1864. The conflicts that ensued between Marx and Bakunin on the role of the state were to provide the basis for a split, and for the ultimate dissolution of the international. The experience of the Second International, established in 1899, was of the inability of parties with revolutionary and reformist orientations to co-exist under the same umbrella, and led to the creation of the Communist International, or COMINTERN, in 1919 (the Third International).

The second experience that was focused on was perhaps what should have been an obvious one: the Spanish Civil War. Its relevance could not be exaggerated, both for where in the world we were sitting at that moment, but also for the fact that fascism is also on the ascendancy in Europe, where it is rearing its ugly head through so-called populist movements and more overtly fascistic groups.

Of course, in contrast to Rojava, the communists and anarchists of 80 years ago often wound up on opposite sides of the barricades. (You can imagine the kind of heated and passionate conversations that took place within my group on this particular issue!)

The sacrifice of more than 25,000 internationalists who perished in the fight for a democratic and progressive Spain free from fascism (which was more than half of the volunteers who came to the country) was not lost on our Kurdish comrades and hundreds have travelled to northern Syria to give up the relative comforts and privileges of their lives at home to fight Daesh's backwardness.

The third example that was given was the bloodiest national liberation war of the twentieth century, which took place in Algeria between 1954 and 1962. On the day that the Second World War ended, the so-called democratic French state drowned the resistance of the Algerian people who were demanding independence in blood, killing 45,000 in a matter of days. Over the course of 8 years of war, more than 1.5 million people were killed, a remarkably heavy toll for the self-determination of a nation.

What was emphasized when our comrades spoke of the Algerian struggle was the fact that a solidarity movement in Europe played a key role in this struggle. Camps were built by solidarity activists in Morocco, for instance, where a factory for ammunition was constructed. The German movement sent out 20,000 letters to members of the French Foreign Legion asking them to change sides – and about 4,000 of them either left or did. The organization Solidarite was founded in order to take care of the financial needs of the National Liberation Front (FLN), and became something of a school for national liberation movements. For instance, they taught South Africa's revolutionaries in the African National Congress how to make fake passports. This example of practical solidarity shows the kind of roles those in the west can play outside of directly aiding the military struggle of revolutionary movements as a combatant.

The war in Vietnam and the social movements that sprang up across the world in response to it was the fourth example provided. Another war of national liberation, the Vietnamese struggle against both French and US imperialism under the leadership of Ho Chi Minh and the Workers' Party of Vietnam was the source of tremendous international solidarity.

In the years of US aggression between 1963 and 1973, more than 2 million Vietnamese perished to bring forward a country that Ho said would be 'ten times more beautiful' when the war ended. The US dropped four times the amount of bombs as it had done in the Second World War. The resistance to the war, not only in the US but across Europe, went hand-in-hand with the global movement of 1968 in the imperialist metropoles. Famously, Che Guevara was to say of Vietnam that such struggles should be waged globally, proclaiming we need 'two, three, many Vietnams'.

The fifth struggle alluded to perhaps had the most practical relevance to the Kurdish revolutionaries for reasons of them being linked at the hip. This was the national liberation movement of the Palestinian people against the Zionist, colonialist state of Israel. It was the Palestine Liberation Organization (PLO) that provided the Kurdish revolutionaries in the PKK with military training at camps in the Bekaa Valley in Lebanon beginning in the late 1970s. Many do not realize that in fact the first shehids (martyrs) of the PKK did not die in combat with the Turkish state, but with the Israeli military. A total of 11 comrades perished in Lebanon in 1982 fighting alongside the PLO, 2 years before the armed struggle was started in Turkey.

The success of Rojava and the increasing interest of revolutionaries to travel there from around the world has led Abdullah Ocalan to say that Rojava should become a centre for world revolution in the twenty-first century similar to what the Bekaa Valley was in the last.

Given this deep connection between the PKK and the Palestinian national liberation movement, it is a cruel irony that often advocates and defenders of narrow Arab nationalism refer in a racist manner to 'the Kurds' as somehow advancing a

Zionist agenda.

Contradictions of War: Ex-Military Fighters and Damned Reds

Although the undogmatic left continues to travel to Rojava to participate in the revolution, and the ideological connections are easy enough to make between the various leftist movements around the world in relation to the leadership in northern Syria, there are also no lack of 'non-ideological' westerners or even reactionaries who have come to join the YPG as well.

There are some quite baffling and absurd accounts of those with right-wing Christian beliefs who came to Syria (presumably to 'kill Muslims') only to be shocked to learn that they were fighting alongside both Muslims and – perhaps scarier for them – those with politics on the far-left of the political spectrum.

Such stories are difficult for me to really grasp since even the most basic internet search could let you know within 2 minutes that the YPG is tied to the 'democratic socialists' of the PYD. This led to the Middle East Eye publishing an article in February 2015 that said, 'Christian Foreign Fighters are deserting the YPG Because They're "Damned Reds".'

As humorous as such headlines and stories might be, they no doubt reflect a very real contradiction. Much of the western left's inability to defend the Rojava Revolution has not only been because of the 'tactical military cooperation' of the YPG/J with the US, but due to the influx of fighters with imperialist military backgrounds joining the YPG.

I asked a YPG commander in Qamishlo about the non-ideological foreign fighters and their ideological orientations and what drives them to fight and die in Rojava when I first arrived in Syria. He told me passionately and without hesitation, 'This isn't the PKK. Here there isn't the luxury of saying, "We will only take you if you adhere to certain ideological principles or are pure." Heval, this is war. In war, there is no time or luxury to build up that kind of military structure. If the YPG tries to be that kind of organization, it will fail.'

Still, I have to concede that I didn't feel so reassured that the revolution was doing all it could to prevent reactionaries from coming to Rojava for their own motivations of living out some war fantasies that were probably wrapped up in having played too many video games as a child. The commander looked at me sternly and said, 'Look, our revolution is one that believes people can change. We wouldn't be having this revolution at all if we didn't believe this, and of course we wouldn't also accept these kind of fighters if we didn't believe they could also be affected by what they see here and change their mentalities.'

It was, like almost everything in Rojava, a statement full of vigour, of passion and of contradiction. It was a statement that also made sense, and seemed to both amplify as well as partially contradict what he had just told me a few minutes before.

My questions to the YPG commander, as well as the answers, struck a chord with me. Before I was a revolutionary Marxist, I was a so-called 'military brat', having grown up mostly on US military bases in Germany and England. I saw the direction that many of my friends decided to go in by following in the footsteps of their parents and joining the army, navy, air force or marines themselves, but my interest in radical ideas as a teenager was already pushing me away from that path. By the age of 18, I identified as a communist, but I will always recall how difficult it was for me to pull myself away from that environment which was the only one I had ever known, or the friendships and connections I lost due to my decision to follow a revolutionary path and attempt to put my ideas into practice – to back up my talk with action.

Therefore, I could understand the commander when he spoke of the movement believing in the power of people to change. I personally went through that process and could relate fully to its intensity, so of course I should also be willing to accept

– and hope that – others could and will also change through the process of fighting side by side with revolutionaries, and possibly become in the truest sense, revolutionists themselves.

Still, the desire for former US, UK, Australian, Canadian and other western military men and women wanting to don the red-star of the YPG and YPJ perplexed me.

I used to spend a great deal of time on the 'Lions of Rojava' Facebook page when it existed. For quite some time, this was the primary way that foreigners who wanted to join the fight against Daesh would get in touch with the YPG to make that a reality. I would never post on the page – I merely observed the type of comments that would be posted to it. Occasionally there was the odd left-winger who expressed interest in joining the fight, but by and large it seemed like ex-military types expressing their will to 'go down range again' and to 'kill ISIS'. Of course, killing ISIS is something I have no issue with – after all, it's the revolutionary duty of the YPG/J to do so to free the people of northern Syria – but I could sense in their words that a not-so-hidden Islamophobia was usually almost ready to emerge. In fact, many of their comments would not be so distant from the kind of words uttered by the new US commander-in-chief Donald Trump in all his racist and bigoted glory.

The YPG has clearly realized over the years of recruiting foreigners that projects like the Lions of Rojava had their limitations and problems. The imagery associated with the project, and the name itself, was one that was quite hyper-masculine, in stark contrast to the reality of the revolution with its feminist and ecological principles. As a result, the project was scrapped.

In its place came the YPG International recruitment initiative. Rather than just sending a message to a Facebook page, the new process means that possible volunteers should at the very least read an orientation about what exactly they are getting themselves into.

The 'About' section on the YPG International website makes clear what the motivations of the volunteer should be, and what the goals of the revolution are, in an attempt to at least mitigate those coming to Rojava to fight who may have less than what one may call 'sincere' intentions:

If you want to support the YPG in Rojava than you should do this for the values of humanity, and not only for your own interest: We don't have money to give you, we don't have fame to give you. What we can give you is the possibility to join an honorable struggle for the values of humanity on the search for the truth and the right way of life and the possibility to learn more about the most important progressive revolution and struggle right now on the planet. What we need are people who want to be part of this for the right reasons. We don't need people who think that they are Rambo or people seeking fame– and please no Fascists. Rojava is not an adventure park, this war is not a Hollywood film and YPG is not a PR-Agency. YPG is also not a place for people which like to kill people because of their nationality, religion, ethnic, sexual or political identity.

My Fellow Americans

The day that I was due to leave northern Iraq to travel to Syria along with some members of my delegation, I crossed paths with a few Americans who were soon to make the journey over the border to join the YPG.

One of them was clearly from the north-east, as his accent gave away a kind of rough edge that I could almost discern as being from, or close to, New York. He approached me when shaking hands with a number of comrades from my group, annunciating his words so clearly and perfectly as if he expected we all knew a sum of zero English. 'I'm from Ameeeriiiiica', he would tell everyone. I shook his hand and with a bit of curiosity

I looked at him sideways and said, 'Yeah, but what part?' As it turned out, he was from New Jersey, and was a former soldier. A wave of contradictory feelings swept over me. Although on the one hand I was trying to undo all of my dogmas and my sectarianism, I instinctively judged this man the very second I found out that he used to wear a US military uniform. I will of course defend my instincts – after all, that uniform has fought against the national liberation struggles and against progressive humanity across the world, from Latin America to the Middle East where I now stood, to south-east Asia.

There was another American with him, someone much more animated, who approached me already wearing a bulletproof vest despite the fact that he wouldn't see combat for at least another month. I thought that surely this was some kind of sick joke. Had I met the real life Rambo?

However, the old adage to never judge a book by its cover it apt, and I was quickly reminded not to be so presumptuous, as I had already made the assumption that this man was also a former imperialist soldier, only to find out that he identified as an anarchist.

I had to do a quick self-reflection and critique here. Of the two Americans I had just met, if I had to guess who exhibited the traits I would usually associate with years of military service, it would be this man. By contrast, the former soldier seemed rather calm, and upon my speaking to him was actually quite critical of his previous experience. As he told me, 'This is the first time I've actually been able to choose where and what to fight for. I've looked into the Kurdish struggle and I can relate to it. I believe in it.'

Honouring the Internationalist Shehids

There is a beautiful monument in the heart of Qamishlo that was unveiled in late 2016 to pay tribute to all of the internationalist fighters who have fallen in the struggle against Daesh and for a new society. Images of these comrades adorn the side of the monument. By the time I was able to visit it, it was already well out of date, as seemingly countless martyrs have given their lives in the anti-fascist fight from lands far away since then.

Returning to my conversation with the YPG commander, I asked him about those who have fallen in this struggle who have come from abroad. He turned to me and said with his characteristic matter-of-fact demeanor, 'This can help address your previous question: If one falls who is non-ideological and one who was a devoted leftist, what difference does it make? They both shed their blood for this cause at the end of the day. They are all shehids because of what they did, not necessarily what ideas they had in their head.'

That being said, the YPG and YPJ do care about crafting the ideas that people have in their heads. The month-long educational programme that is part of the training for a new recruit is testament to this. Not only are there military lessons, but it can be said that the bulk of the process is actually about receiving ideological education.

As the homepage of YPG International makes clear:

YPG strives for a democratic, ecologic, and anti-patriarchal system of self-organisation; it takes its power from the people and fights for the people. We struggle to defend the dignity of being a human when there is no one around to defend it and to create an ethico-political society in order to realize ideals of equality, justice, freedom, and self-determination. We wage a war against all forms of fascism and capitalist hegemony that try to enslave the peoples and destroy the nature. We get our inspiration from the philosophy of Abdullah Ocalan whose ideas have become a torch in the jungle of oppression for the poor and the downtrodden; not only in Kurdistan but also in all around the world.

It's this world outlook and the internationalism of the movement that will help it continue to grow and to garner the attention of progressive-minded people from every corner of the world.

It was the reason that German revolutionary Ivana Hoffman joined the MLKP, fought side by side with the YPJ, and gave her life to the revolution at just 19 years young, fighting and falling as a shehid under her Kurdish name Avasin. This internationalist perspective was the same one that provided the motivation for American socialist Michael Israel to join the IFB. He was murdered in a Turkish airstrike in late 2016, known to his comrades as Robin Agiri. Before becoming a shehid, he had posted on social media:

> The Rojava struggle is the most dynamic and ground breaking revolutionary movement of our time. I am determined that it is the job of leftist allies and internationalists to rally behind this movement, to help build it up and learn from it. Things that we may have only dreamed of in theoretical writing are acted upon in Rojava, modified and adapted to their struggle and made real. Rojava is doing this all and reorganizing society despite the chaos and destruction of 5 years of civil war. The gains of the revolution under such austere and harsh conditions is truly remarkable. Now that I am back in Rojava, I know all my needs will be met. Here I will never be in want of basic necessities for lack of money. I, like all others in Rojava, will never go without food and water, clothing or a place to rest my head at night. The movement takes care of people here. That is not to say though that Rojava and the rest of Syria do not need help though. I'm calling on all of my friends and comrades to learn about the Rojava revolution and how they have been leading the charge in the war against ISIS fascists. I'm calling on all of you who are able, to do your part in helping or sending donations so that this revolution may become stronger with the aid of the international community.

His call has since been answered by countless other internationalists, some of whom have since also been eternalized as martyrs for a better world. The sacrifice of those like Michael continues a proud, militant tradition of global solidarity written in blood before it by the shehids of yesterday, staining the red flag of the world's workers and oppressed that we will always hold high.

Chapter 9

Ocalan's Ideology: Establishing a Multi-Ethnic, Democratic Society

When the liberation of Raqqa was announced on 17 October 2017, the revolutionary forces of the YPG and YPJ didn't hesitate to dedicate this monumental victory to the ideological leader of the Kurdish Freedom Movement, Abdullah Ocalan. For those who had sacrificed everything and risked their lives to see the capital of Daesh's so-called caliphate brought under the control of a socialist, feminist movement, there was no greater motivating force than the example of their imprisoned leader, known affectionately and with great fondness as Serok Apo.

During my trip to Syria more than 6 months beforehand, I had heard Ocalan's name mentioned in countless ideological discussions and educationals. There was no doubt that he was the leader of this revolutionary process despite being locked away in solitary confinement on the Imrali Island off Istanbul for nearly 2 decades, and having no direct input on the decisions undertaken by the movement.

Dozens of YPG and YPJ members told me of how the US was hoping to help 'liberalize' the movement by trying to convince certain elements behind the revolution to 'let Apo down' and push his philosophy to the background. Time and time again, the hevals asserted that Ocalan's ideas were indispensable to their fight and that they would never be disloyal to his concepts and principles, and that peace in the Middle East was ultimately impossible without his freedom. He was their Nelson Mandela, a figure whose imprisonment only deepened the loyalty of the cadres of the movement to his leadership.

Yet, it wasn't only the US that was vexed at the sight of a massive banner of Ocalan soon being unveiled in the heart of the former Daesh caliphate. Narrow Arab nationalists also used the opportunity to accuse the Kurdish Freedom Movement, quite ironically, of its own nationalism. They attacked this move on behalf of the YPG and YPJ as evidence of a colonial land-grab backed by imperialist war planes. In their view, this was evidence of Kurdish occupation, despite the fact that the Kurdistan Workers' Party (PKK) and its associated organizations had left Kurdish nationalism and the desire for a nation-state aside by the mid-2000s with the adoption of the party's new paradigm that called for autonomy and the democratic nation.

Ocalan has been clear that the establishment of a Kurdish nation-state would create as many problems as it would solve, offering instead a solution based on each ethnic group and community being able to freely organize itself in communes and cooperatives, and with its own self-defence forces.

West of the Euphrates

Raqqa would not be the first experiment in, or test of, the ability of the democratic confederalist movement advocated by Ocalan and led by Kurdish forces to bring Arab and other communities into the emancipatory project offered by the movement. Throughout Rojava, the Arab-only road signs that previously existed have either been replaced or are now side by side with ones written in Arabic, Kurdish and Assyrian. These signs reflect the cultural diversity of the region, and the multi-lingual nature of it. They are also part of a concerted attempt to put into practice the fight against ethnic chauvinism. Kurdish narrow nationalism cannot replace the bigotry and racism of Arab nationalism. Fears of an 'independent' Kurdish-dominated mini-state in the north of the country are misplaced and have no basis in reality.

When the YPG and YPJ began to push back against and to strangle the Daesh pseudo-caliphate by scoring victories that shrunk the territory held by the fascists, they began to move into areas in which Kurds were a minority and Arabs the majority.

One of these struggles would unfold in the battle for the city of Manbij, which had initially been taken by elements of the so-called Syrian opposition grouped in the FSA in 2012, before falling to Daesh in January 2014. In June of 2016, after more than 2 years under the control of Baghdadi's reign of darkness and terror, the YPG/J-led SDF announced the start of a campaign to free the city. Rather than coordinate its operation directly under the red, gold and green flags associated with Kurdish nationhood, however, the SDF forces concluded that a new Manbij Military Council should be established that would mean a leadership representative of the city being tasked with administering military affairs both during the battle as well as post-liberation. Such a council isn't unique, as an al-Bab Military Council and Jarablus Military Council have also been established.

When the city was freed on 12 August after 2 months of fighting, the SDF transferred full control to the Manbij Military Council and to the newly established Manbij Civilian Council which would have the responsibility of pushing forward reconstruction and for the implementation of direct democracy and gender equality.

During my visit to Syria, I hadn't expected to be able to visit a place like Manbij, which at that time had only been freed from the grip of Daesh for a little over 7 months.

Laying west of the Euphrates River, Manbij – along with al-Bab and Jarablus – was a major point of contention between the SDF, Turkey and the US. The advancement of Kurdish-led forces over the Euphrates meant the very real possibility that they would soon be able to link the cantons of Cizire and Kobane with Afrin, which would mean the autonomous, self-declared federation straddling the Syrian-Turkish border would see its three cantons linked. This was the worst nightmare of the fascists of the AKP and Sultan Erdogan, who pressured the US to demand that units of the YPG and YPJ withdraw east of the Euphrates after the liberation of Manbij. Although these assurances had been given, and the movement pointed to the independence of the Manbij Civilian and Military Councils from the YPG, YPJ or PYD, Ankara would consistently claim that Kurdish forces still dominated the city and surrounding areas.

As such, I thought it impossible that I would be able to travel west of the 'Firat' to areas that were not considered 'Rojava' – as they weren't Kurdish – but which were still deemed to be part of the new democratic confederalist project and federation.

However, upon arriving in Kobane from Qamishlo after a drive of more than 6 hours across the stunning terrain that sits on the Syria-Turkey border, I received word that our group would be able to have exclusive access to Manbij the following day. I couldn't believe how fortunate I was – after all, it was one thing to witness the largely 'Kurdish revolution', but this would provide an important opportunity to see if the movement was successful in organizing the Arab population, or if major hurdles and contradictions still presented themselves.

The sight of the serene and glistening Euphrates is one that can't be put into words. It becomes inconceivable to imagine that such a gorgeous sight has been home to the world's most bitter war for the last half decade.

It doesn't take long to drive from the outskirts of Kobane to the Euphrates, although as soon as one travels across the river, the landscape changes considerably. It seems inexplicable. Suddenly the amount of greenery, of trees, of vibrancy, intensifies. How could it all appear so different? As our heval guides told us, this was due to the fact that in Kurdish areas, the planting of trees was previously banned by the Ba'ath government. It's not until one enters largely Arab-inhabited territory that the discriminatory practises that had been put in place until 2012 appeared so evident. This was a radically different world. It suddenly dawned on me why when I was in Qamishlo a few days before, the comrades had put such major emphasis on the planting of trees, which they had dedicated to the freedom of

Ocalan.

Before we entered the city of Manbij, we were told that we would be taking a slight detour in order to see some of the impressive cultural heritage that the area had to offer. We approached the world-renowned Qal'at Najm, a castle that sits on the banks of the Euphrates and which has been featured in Arab literature since the seventh century.

As our van approached the entrance to this castle, a man who had to have been in his late 50s or early 60s greeted us with the most enthusiastic smile I had seen in weeks. He eagerly shook our hands, his radiant glow never leaving his face, and grabbed his keys to open the gates to what was truly a historical treasure. He then appeared as if he was almost in tears. He assumed that we were all 'tourists', which in some sense was true on this particular day, although none of us had the heart to either then or later tell him that we were on an internationalist delegation of solidarity activists and journalists. He had been facilitating tours to this castle for decades, and spoke with deep and profound sadness about how it had been years since anyone had come to stay at his home adjacent to the castle which he had offered as lodging for tourists from across the world. He pointed out how Daesh had used the castle as a point of defence during the war due to its strategic position on the river, but they had quickly abandoned it when their defeat appeared imminent.

We spent more than an hour walking through the massive structure, looking with awe at what was such an impressive construction, amazed that after the tumultuous history it had experienced, it remained intact. More than this, we were grateful to see the optimism and joy of this tour guide who looked forward with great enthusiasm to the revival of the tourism industry in his homeland.

A few hours later, as we entered the city of Manbij, it became apparent that this was a thriving community that exhibited – at least outwardly – few noticeable scars of war. The streets bustled with markets selling fruits, vegetables, kebabs, clothing, appliances. There didn't seem to be a war economy in effect here, although this of course was impossible for me to say with certainty given that I was forming my own subjective opinions based on limited information, and rather quick first impressions.

What was certain though, is that just after half a year after the darkness of Daesh rule had been lifted, people were getting on with life. Just a little over a week before my visit on 12 March 2017, the Legislative Assembly of Manbij approved 13 new committees to administer the city that included 71 Arabs, 43 Kurds, 10 Turkmen, 8 Circassians, an Armenian and a Chechen. As my guides told me, although Arabs made up the majority of the population here, there were considerable communities of ethnic minorities. It was said that the Kurdish people here had been much more Arabized that in the communities where they made up the majority such as Kobane or in the Cizire canton, and the same was true for a substantial part of the Armenian population. This was seen as largely an essential part of surviving in a country that only recognized one nation, one flag, one identity.

What was striking about the stories of the liberation of the city was the enthusiasm with which a number of Arab women had joined the ranks of the Manbij Military Council. We met a woman of only 17 who had lived her entire life only 15 minutes from the city, in the area between the historic castle and the metropolis. Yet, she had never before entered the city, and prior to joining the liberation forces she had expected that her role in life would be nothing more than being a housewife. Now, her first time entering Manbij was with an AK-47 swung over her shoulder and her head held up high. Her freedom was taken, not only from the tyrannical forces of the so-called Islamic State, but from the regressive and reactionary cultural norms of tradition which had dictated society until the principles of Ocalan's philosophy began to make their way into her society, changing her life and those of her community forever.

Retreating back over the Euphrates to the east, the comrades pointed out a historical curiosity – the fact that there is a piece of land that the Republic of Turkey still claims as its own. The sight of Kurdish men and women in military fatigues pointing to the location that previously held a 40-man garrison of Turkish troops who guarded the tomb of Suleyman Shah was deeply ironic. In the early months of 2015, as the liberation of Kobane had been accomplished, Turkish forces entered Syrian territory to evacuate their men and move the location of the tomb, a move that was declared a flagrant act of aggression by the Syrian government. Turkey still claims the territory that held the old tomb as its own, as is hardly surprising given the colonialist and expansionist Ottoman dreams of Erdogan and his cohorts.

In stark contrast to Turkey's nationalism as well as the narrow nationalism of Syrian Arabism, the model espoused by Abdullah Ocalan has shown itself able to take root not only in Kurdish communities, but across ethnic divides. Of course, chauvinism refined and perpetuated over generations doesn't vanish overnight. It would be flawed to say that such attitudes don't exist in Kurdish, Arab, Assyrian, Armenian or Turkmen society, or even among cadres involved in the building of the new society.

As was alluded to countless times during my stay in Syria, 10 per cent of the battle is military, 90 per cent is internal. Overcoming such prejudices is part and parcel of this great battle, which is the primary struggle in crafting a new social, political and economic order. However, with revolutionary optimism, diligence, patience and persistence, such a heterogenous and diverse democratic is slowly coming to life in and outside of the territory of Rojava, shining as a radical example of potential and hope in the aftermath of fascist rule.

Chapter 10

Communes and Cooperatives: The Basis of Rojava's Society

Much of Abdullah Ocalan's theoretical writings in the aftermath of his kidnapping and subsequent incarceration in 1999 have focused on developing the PKK's new paradigm of 'libertarian' socialism and democratic confederalism. These writings and the ideological vision have contributed much to the debate within the radical left in the period of demoralization and then re-groupment which followed the collapse of the Soviet Union and eastern bloc socialist states in the 1989-91 period. Ocalan's views on the subject are no doubt controversial, as his aim is clearly to distance the PKK not only from the history of twentieth-century socialist projects, but also from the organization's own Leninist past.

While I believe that the global left in general owes Ocalan a great historic debt for taking up the process of deeply analyzing what factors contributed to the fall of 'actually existing socialism' at the end of the last century, I don't always find his arguments convincing. I believe, for instance, that his approach towards some historical examples that are found in the first two volumes of his *Prison Writings* lack proper material and historical context. In short, I believe some of his work comes close to essentially 'throwing the baby out with the bathwater', playing up Leninism's apparent failures and refusing to acknowledge many of its massively transforming achievements, particularly for women's rights and liberation.

This isn't to say that his mission isn't correct; I believe the many evident shortcomings and contradictions of the twentieth-century Marxist-Leninist states, particularly their democratic deficits, need thorough analyzing. It's also important to consider that his *Prison Writings* were written as an appeal to the European Court of Human Rights, perhaps important to mention when considering the content that plays on the 'democratic' nature of the European Union.

How thorough Ocalan's theoretical breaks have been in practice is also a question of great debate. One can argue that little has actually changed in terms of party organization that would separate it from the traditional Leninist model, despite the new, seemingly eclectic views of Serok Apo. What is undoubtedly true is that the ideological shift of the Kurdish Freedom Movement has led to opposing views among the radical left in terms of what this new paradigm represents. Is it a historical retreat in the face of socialism's near-total collapse globally and the apparent temporary victory of the international capitalism system? Is it genuine, or merely a tactical change in order to help garner more support for the cause? Is it completely throwing in the towel to liberalism and shedding any true revolutionary convictions entirely?

The latter argument has been taken up by many critiques of not only Ocalan and the PKK, but of the fraternal Rojava Revolution being advanced by the PYD and TEV-DEM since 2012. Many western Marxists in particular have refused to support the struggle of the PYD and its military wings, the YPG and YPJ, because they apparently lack a 'socialist' character.

Part of my trip to Rojava was focused on the question of the economy, ownership, public participation and other key questions related to the ideology of the revolution. To put it succinctly, I wanted to analyze whether this revolution had any true socialist characteristics, or if it was more akin to a democratic national liberation struggle. A thorough look at the system of communes and cooperatives is beyond the intended scale of this book. However, I can share some of the experiences I had in Rojava with these structures that can hopefully contribute to a greater understanding of what they represent, as well as the successes they have achieved and problems that are confronting the revolutionary forces.

A War Economy

The first thing that I believe is indispensable to remember when looking at the current economic state of Rojava is that this is a war economy.

More than 5 years after the proclamation of autonomy, despite the increased amount of territory that the federation has managed to achieve and the relative peace that has taken root particularly in Cizire and Kobane cantons, the bulk of the economic resources of the cantons continue to go towards the war effort. This undoubtedly means that projects that are envisioned by political leaders and the masses of people alike are largely put on hold until the material circumstances allow them to be put into effect – in other words, when the enemies of the revolution have been defeated and peace finally reigns again.

One of the most stifling ways that the war economy is manifested is through the blockade that has been enforced by the reactionary, collaborationist regime of Barzani's KDP in northern Iraq. This led to a situation where when the revolutionaries in Rojava decided to upend decades of Arab nationalist policy of not allowing the refining of the oil found in the region, they were forced to smuggle the equipment needed for the refinery in small parts via backpacks across the border rather than have it delivered in one go.

The embargo is a ruthless and harmful practice on behalf of the KDP government, but in a spirit that was embodied in the Cuban people when the US imposed its blockade on the island beginning in 1961, it has also led to great ingenuity and creativity for the people of northern Syria to become more self-sufficient.

The Example of Two Cooperatives

This spirit is evident at the 'Roj Av' water factory near Dirbesiye in the Cizire canton, which like all major industries is a cooperative (the name of the brand is a clever play on words, as 'av' means water). The factory employs dozens of men and women, who all have an equal say in the daily operations of the cooperative, a far cry from the employer-employee relationship prevalent in our societies. There are managers at the factory, but they are recallable by democratic vote and lack the kind of power to dictate affairs to the other workers. Their role is simply to take greater responsibility for certain administrative tasks. As Heval Sores, who helps to manage the cooperative, says, 'We have the goal to build a new kind of society, not only in our homes, but in our factories. People here are enthusiastic about their work because they feel as if they are co-owners, not subjects who just receive a wage and then go home.'

While the goal of the cooperative is to ultimately become self-sufficient and to avoid any kind of dependence on sources outside of Syria for the materials needed for the bottling of water, such a reality is currently outside the means of possibility. This has led to an extremely difficult and precarious situation for the drivers who risk their lives to bring the plastic that is used for the bottles through Syria via Lebanon. Such a trip means traversing through territory held by the Syrian government, Arab opposition forces and often Salafi Islamist groups. Yet, the result of such a brave mission is that Rojava can manufacture its own bottled water, a move towards self-sufficiency even if the end goal is still far from being realized.

Several kilometres to the south of the factory lies an agricultural cooperative that employs 5,000 people on land that was previously nationalized and owned by the Syrian Arab state. As one of their charismatic and youthful members tells me:

Although the land was supposed to be the common property

of the people, that wasn't the reality. It was very unproductive. People felt no degree of ownership at all. This has changed now. We have a system where anybody who wants to join can do so by contributing $100. If they can't afford this, we can find a way around it that works for the cooperative and the individual. After the first year, we normally invest 25 per cent of our earnings back into the cooperative. The profits are split evenly, and everyone works a minimum of one week per year on this land.

I was eager to know if this model meant that there were problems of inequality despite the even pay outs for each member. For instance, were there not some cooperative members who put in more work than others? Furthermore, how was leadership determined? I was told that, 'Leadership changes every 2 years, and of course anybody is recallable before that if they are deemed to not be sufficiently carrying out the role that they were entrusted with. Of course, some members of the cooperative work harder than others do. Our meetings have been helpful in resolving problems related to a lack of work ethic, however.'

On the surface, the water and agricultural cooperatives certainly appeared to function well. It was clear that the primary reason for this was the feeling among members that they weren't merely workers, but that the destiny of the project was in their hands. They felt a sense of ownership they previously hadn't. The means of production and the land had been democratized, freeing many from the drudgery of life they had known all too well before this process began to unfold.

Self-Sufficiency and Foreign Trade
One of the key questions I had about the general economic vision of the federation was how it would handle the process of construction, reconstruction and development of the region's industrial capabilities. The north-east of Syria had previously

been kept intentionally undeveloped as a consequence of Arabization policies. However, now that self-administration had been achieved, how would the democratic management of the economy by the Kurds, Arabs, Turkmen, Assyrians and other nationalities actually develop?

A certain curiosity I had was on how self-sufficient the federation would aspire to be, and what this meant for international trade. I spoke with Heval Serhildan, one of the economic ministers for the Cizire canton, about these issues. He was quick to point out firstly that Rojava couldn't view itself as independent from the rest of Syria. The goal had to be to develop the economy of the canton and the federation along with that of the rest of the country. He also pointed out that although they had a view to developing industry, this wouldn't be done similarly to the kind of mass industrialization that a capitalist economy would perhaps be prone to pursuing. 'We have to consider the ecological impact of all of our development decisions. Development that comes at a cost to our environment isn't really development at all.'

Still, would the canton or the federation agree to international investment? Would this make the imperialists wide-eyed and encourage them to rush in, perhaps undermining the central principles of the revolution?

'In principle, we have nothing against investment. But, our model will mean that if we enter into partnerships with companies that wish to invest, we need to maintain 51 per cent ownership. Furthermore, companies won't be able to come in to exploit people or to engage in hazardous practices.'

The model seemed familiar, in line with the development strategy put forward by Cuba during the special period of 1991-97, when a wave of hotel building was done through joint ventures that used this 51-49 formula. I got the sense that although the leadership was aware that development was needed, there was also a desire to tread very carefully and cautiously, and to not allow the core values of the revolution – democracy, equality, ecology – to be sacrificed.

Viva La Commune

While the cooperative is the backbone of the new Rojavan economy, it's the commune that dominates social relations. One of Ocalan's most thorough critiques of the experience of socialism in the twentieth century was the rampant bureaucratism, or people's democratic will being stifled in the name of people themselves. As such, the Rojava Revolution, like the autonomous project initiated in parts of northern Kurdistan as well as Shengal, has taken very seriously the construction of a bottom-up kind of system that allows for mass participation and debate at the most basic levels of society. This didn't appear to me to be radically different from the approach of Venezuela's Hugo Chavez when he proclaimed the need for a twenty-first century socialism to be more participatory and inclusive of the poor and working people.

I was able to visit an academy in Derik (al-Malikiyah) near the Syria-Iraq border to discuss the commune structure with comrades who were involved in the development of these structures there. I was told that in Derik, there were 29 communes, each consisting of between 100 and 300 families. Together, these communes made up the city council that took decisions for administration from below. In the entire area including the surrounding villages, there were 104 communes. These villages form their own village councils, and together with the city council they comprise a regional council. This seemed to be a system of direct democracy in which no single family or person was left outside of the realm of decision making, and leaders were chosen in the most democratic of ways.

Characteristic of the Kurdish Freedom Movement's policy of advancing gender equality and women's liberation, each commune chose co-presidents (one man and one woman).

Within the commune, 12 committees worked on various aspects of neighbourhood policy: municipal affairs, parastin (defence), economy, press, families of shehids, arts and culture, diplomacy, workers, education, health care, ideology and justice. There are often sub-committees within the committees themselves. For instance, the municipal affairs committee includes sub-committees responsible for ecology and price controls.

I'm told that everybody living in a neighbourhood is automatically part of a commune, and their participation cannot be denied. However, some elements of society who identify more with the conservative and regressive politics of the KDP and Barzani have refused to participate, although they have been encouraged to do so. Despite this, participation is voluntary, and nobody is forced to join meetings of the commune. Every active member of the commune engaged in political and ideological education, including those from professions such as doctors, judges and teachers. There is no hierarchy or ability for someone to skip this process because they are deemed to be too important.

On the second Friday of every month, the communes meet and the participation of at least one family member is requested. On the day of elections for the commune, everybody is informed well in advance. I was told that there is no distinction made between ethnic groups in the commune model, and the combating of ethnic chauvinism is a key part of the work taken on by the ideological committees. Also, there may be more than one role for a member of a commune to play. For instance, it is common that a comrade might be involved in arts and culture, but also is a member of the HPC, or People's Defence Force. As one enthusiastic commune member told me, 'I'm not only singing and dancing, but taking the rifle and defending the neighbourhood.'

In line with what I had been told when asking about the cooperative structure, the comrades drove home the idea of how important popular and mass participation was in the development of a free and sovereign society. 'If we don't develop our own society, somebody else will' was a common saying.

Mediation is an important part of the commune's work conducted by the justice committee. This means that contradictions between tribes, land disputes and other issues that may traditionally have been handled either in courts or through other means are now the work of the commune. I was told that in Derik in 2016, 90 per cent of these kinds of conflicts were able to be resolved through such structures rather than in courts, a major accomplishment for this democratic model.

The comrades were honest about the shortcomings associated with the structures, however. For instance, it was pointed out that many of the communes still lack an active arts and culture committee, which may exist on paper but have yet to actually put on events that will help to build the indigenous cultural life of the community. Also, one comrade said bluntly about the health committees, 'This may lag behind for 50 years because of the war and the brain drain. We don't have many doctors remaining here anymore. This will be a long and meticulous process.'

Another issue that is prevalent seems to be the idea that a lot of people still 'don't get it'. This is said to be the result of the new system being so radically different from anything the society knew before. Almost overnight, people had the ability to wield power in their own hands rather than be dictated to on what to do or how to live. This is a problem that the comrades are sure will eventually be overcome, but which will continue to take patience and persistence to solve. As one young woman tells me, 'When people see the necessity of joining this democratic system, then we will have a truly successful system.'

Optimism for the Future

How Rojava's future develops is far from a resolved issue. Will its democratic, multi-ethnic revolution continue to deepen and advance towards a twenty-first century socialism that reflects the best of the last century's tradition combined with a critical spirit and more liberatory framework? Will the non-state model advocated by the movement actually be able to resist the pressures of not only imperialist penetration but of more liberal elements who wish to pursue a different course in the federation? Will a political settlement mean that peace will prevail and the full potential of the Rojavan project will finally sprout?

It's been a century now since the first time the working-class anywhere in the world took state power and held it. The October Revolution of 1917 that brought the downtrodden of Petrograd to power and would usher in the Soviet Union several years later showed humanity the potential of the oppressed to govern themselves. However, the war waged against the Bolsheviks by 14 imperialist powers and internal counter-revolutionary forces, as well as the isolation the Soviets faced as a result of the inability of other European revolutionary movements to overthrow their respective capitalist governments, meant the world's first socialist state developed very differently from the way that Lenin imagined it would. Such material analysis is always needed. It's important when we look at the Soviet Union, the socialist states that continue to exist and the Rojava project.

Considering the suffocation that has been imposed on the Democratic Federation of Northern Syria thus far by the Kurdish collaborationists, the Turkish state and the monstrosity of Daesh, as well as the pressures imposed by the result of tactical cooperation with the US, the results to date are nothing short of miraculous. Yet, the stuff of miracles is the result of decades of movement building and slow ideological and practical work. The world's progressive people owe it to themselves to learn from and study the Rojava Revolution, as well as to lend it support and solidarity at this critical juncture. Failure to do so will undoubtedly be to the detriment of the world's oppressed, colonized and downtrodden yearning to be free.

Chapter 11

Shehid Namirin: To Live Like the Fallen Will Be Humanity's Revenge

Death is of course a major, indeed fundamental, part of war. No revolutionary struggle worthy of the name can be fought, and certainly not won, without a tremendous degree of sacrifice in which humanity's most precious sons and daughters often live for what only seems like a flash. The young are the ones to not only make revolution, but to carry the burden of often not living to see it made. Their moment in history in terms of years spent on the earth seems even more insignificant than those who live 'full lives' of 80 or 90 years. Yet, their often exceptionally brief time on this planet – because of their ultimate sacrifice – manifests in deaths that, to echo what Mao Zedong once said, are heavier than Mount Tai in contrast to the reactionaries whose deaths are lighter than feathers.

Kurdish culture is one in which mountains have a key significance, so the idea of the Chinese revolutionary conveyed more than half a century ago is one that I'm certain has some degree of relevance for a modern revolutionary struggle half way across the world. It is often said, after all, that Kurds have no friends except these mountains.

The number of young warriors who are taken from this world at an appallingly young age in conflict is almost impossible to conceive of in the contexts of the relative comfort of western society today. The struggles of the twentieth century bear out just how much blood had to be spilled onto the battlefields of Asia, Africa and Latin America in struggles that were principally about national liberation, not to mention the Second World War in which up to 27 million Soviets gave their lives to smash fascism. A total of 1.5 million perished in Algeria to boot out the supposedly democratic French state. Millions more died in Indochina to kick out the same initial colonizer, and later the US. Struggles in Africa against the Portuguese, Spanish, British and French claimed millions more.

We know all too well the optimistic and romantic revolutionary sentiments associated with such monumental suffering. Che Guevara once said it didn't matter if he fell anywhere in the world as long as another comrade came to pick up his gun. It was an idea I was to hear repeated throughout my time in Rojava.

The last thing I really want to do is romanticize the idea of death. Frankly, it's extremely difficult to know how to really write about it because the culture of the shehid, or martyr, in Kurdistan seems so far removed from our lifestyles. Images everywhere of those who have given their lives for a cause much bigger than themselves was something I first encountered in Palestine when I visited the West Bank in 2010. At that time, I remember commenting to a friend of mine that the volume of posters that were omnipresent seemed similar to what in our society would be movie posters, or those promoting musical artists or concerts. They lined the streets of cities like Nablus and Jenin, and I could only imagine what growing up not only under occupation, but with images like that all around you, does to a young child psychologically.

In Kurdistan, my experience was very similar. If anything, because of the high level of warfare currently taking place, the posters and images were even more omnipotent. The streets of every city and town were lined with photos of young men and women of the YPG and YPJ, the majority of whom I'm sure were considerably younger than I am today when they were martyred.

Admittedly, I'm shaking a bit while writing this. I have to confess that I feel at a major loss as to how to speak about death at this moment because even though my visit to Rojava was relatively brief, there were a number of comrades who I met who would soon thereafter fall.

Perhaps 'fall' isn't the right word – it is more fitting to say they were killed in the most disgusting and merciless way by the fascist Turkish state. These were comrades who just days ago fell victim to the airstrikes committed by Turkey in Mount Karachok, not far from the city of Derik in Cizire canton. These saw 22 human beings taken from us in a flash in the early hours of the morning of 25 April in what the AKP government said was an operation to prevent the PKK from sending logistics into Turkey. The truth is that the comrades who perished were fighting against the largest fascist threat the world has seen in recent memory, Daesh. In addition to bombing Syria, Turkey also carried out attacks in Shengal in Iraq. It's a fitting portrayal of the role of Turkey to see images of Shengal in the aftermath of these airstrikes – one of the places targeted was the martyrs' cemetery where fighters who fell in combat defending the local Yezidi population against the so-called Islamic State are resting. Even in death, they haven't known peace, as Erdogan's forces bombed their graves. Daesh would undoubtedly be proud.

The feeling to know that some of the most warm and humble human beings you have ever had the honour to shake hands with, eat and drink with and spend precious peaceful time getting to know could so quickly thereafter be killed in the most heinous of ways is disturbing, eerie and provokes feelings of sadness and rage.

But not despair, at least not in my case. Of course, the idea that any of our heroes or heroines could die at any moment was always there. They all spoke about that possibility, and in some cases, even the eventuality of it taking place. I suppose that once you commit to joining the YPG or YPJ and put on your fatigues, you have also committed to the idea that you may not live to see the conclusion of the war, or the ability of the children of your generation to grow up in a radically different society. It still doesn't make losing anybody any easier, though. Once you get that news, it eats at your heart, and seems to puncture a part of your soul.

I don't mean to sound like I'm making this about me – but at this point, I feel like all I can really offer is my subjective analysis and my emotional response. I know that I have the luxury of living outside of the Syrian war zone. I felt a certain sense of guilt for even leaving Rojava, even though the expectation from the beginning was that I would only be there for a short period of time. It's hard not to feel like my trip there wasn't anything more than revolutionary tourism – I'll be trying hard to do all I can to change that through my contributions, but something tells me at least in part those feelings will never really change.

I recall the words of an internationalist woman fighter who I had the privilege to get to know, if only very briefly, while in Syria. She conveyed to me a common sentiment among the YPJ and the movement, in general, about commitment and sacrifice. She told me in her characteristic soft-spoken manner, 'I had to come back to Rojava [after going home for a few months] because anything else seems like I've committed treason. Even if we don't live to see the end of this war and the society we want to build, others will, and that makes dying here worth it.'

Sentiments like that – as well as the monumental level of commitment that internationalist comrades like her have made – reveal in part the psychology of war, but more than that what it means to fight with conviction. It's the main reason that 'the Kurds' in the Syrian context have been the most effective force against Daesh despite for so long having been rather primitively equipped with 4-decade old Kalashnikovs and a lack of body armour. The reason why they win on the battlefield is because the battle of ideas has already been won in their minds and hearts. Nothing can stop a force equipped with that degree of willpower.

The morning that the news of the Karachok attack was making its rounds in the international media, I felt heartbroken to realize that I knew not only the location of the attack – as it had been the last place I visited in Syria – but also several of the fallen hevals. One of these was a YPJ fighter known as Destan.

She had left a lasting impression on me when I met her in Derik along with her siblings. I remember that they all teased me as to why I hadn't learned Kurdish yet (I tried my best to insist that 2 weeks in the country wasn't long enough to pick up the language). She was curious about the revolutionary struggle in the US, and through translation we managed to have some fascinating conversations. Her words about the YPJ have stayed with me, and it was these sentences that I remembered upon seeing her face across the internet, emblazoned on a shehid poster: 'There are actually similarities between the YPG and YPJ and Daesh. I mean that in the sense that we both fight without fear. But while Daesh fights because they want to die – to go to paradise – we fight because we have something to live for.'

It was a moment to be remembered, like so many on a daily basis in Rojava. It wasn't just what she said, but the manner in which she said it. This wasn't just propaganda that was spat out by the party, absorbed by its cadres and then spat out on an individual level. This was something she truly believed. Even with the language barrier obviously causing some issues in terms of understanding, body language doesn't lie. Her sincerity in everything she said and did was beyond dispute.

Heval Destan's death is a blow to humanity. I mean that not just poetically, or because it sounds romantic, or because I want to exaggerate her significance. Her demise at the hands of Erdogan's anti-women government was an attack upon the women's liberation movement globally. The Kurdish struggle is very adamant about their revolution being about more than just the liberation of 'their' people, but being the vanguard struggle for the entire planet. It's an assessment I agree with, and Destan's words in an interview she conducted a few years ago retain their validity today, even after her murder: 'I hope that Kurdish women can inspire women all over the world. We are not only fighting for Kurdish women but for women all over the world.'

I don't truly know how to do justice to the legacy of the comrades like Destan and the countless others who have been taken from us prematurely either at the hands of the reactionary Turkish state or the faux-caliphate of Daesh. I'm reminded of something that was said to me on numerous occasions in Rojava about who is and who isn't a revolutionary. Even those I encountered who have been committed members of the Kurdish revolutionary movement for decades did not regard themselves as revolutionaries. I asked one YPG fighter why they refused to identify themselves this way. 'Well, you have to see it this way. The only ones we see as revolutionaries are the shehids. We know that they died revolutionaries. Until one does, there is the chance they will abandon or betray the revolution. But the shehids never committed treason. They stayed true to the end.'

Heval Destan, as well as the other 21 murdered at Mount Karachok, were the truest of revolutionaries. It is a path to aspire to, not only for those living and fighting in Rojava, but for the whole of progressive humanity. To live by the values and ethics of the society that we desire to create will be our revenge in the face of the forces of darkness.

Chapter 12

Heval Demhat's Blood Now Nourishes the Soil

In the early morning hours of the day I was supposed to return from northern Iraq to Europe after spending more than a month in Mesopotamia, I suddenly and violently woke up in a state of panic. I've been prone to having quite intense nightmares for the past several years of my life, so that itself wouldn't have been anything particularly unusual. However, on this occasion I woke up with the assumption that I was no longer alive, even uttering to myself, 'I actually did die!' After standing up and at least partially waking myself up, I was able to stop the process of hyperventilating and came to the conclusion that I was alive and well. I turned on the light by the dresser and glanced at my bed and my backpack, seeing my clothes sprawled out across the room exactly as I had left them a few hours before.

Was this some kind of post-traumatic stress disorder from having just returned from a warzone? I'm not entirely sure, but it's no doubt possible. I was beginning the process of adjusting to being in a place where I no longer felt the need to maintain the strictest vigilance 24 hours a day. This surely wouldn't be an overnight process.

A part of me had to accept before travelling to Syria – presently one of the most dangerous countries on the face of the planet – that there was the chance that something could happen to me that would mean I wouldn't return home. This was despite the fact that I was travelling there in a civilian capacity and not to join the ranks of the YPG. Still, the thought of travelling to such volatile terrain provoked very strong emotional and psychological responses ahead of me packing my bag to leave Europe for the region. I didn't know how to adequately deal with the feelings that I was about to do something that I considered border-line risky. This led to confused thoughts about how to speak with my partner about the trip and how dangerous it could possibly be. Although she was supportive of me doing something that I had said several times 'I just have to do', she was understandably somewhat apprehensive. So was I, even if I tried to ignore or deny those troubling feelings.

Six weeks later, I was alive and well, full of militant fervour, already missing the comrades I had left behind in Rojava. Despite not yet being back in Europe, I was already plotting my return to Syria for some point in the not too distant future. So here I was, in a small yet comfortable room in Sulaymaniyah, lying awake at 2:30 in the morning on the verge of going home to all of my comforts and my petit-bourgeoisie existence. I recalled how it was more than 1 month before when I had sat in this same room before travelling across the Iraq-Syria border, a time when the excitement, anxiety and uncertainty of what lay before me was consuming.

When the News Hits and the Grief Follows

Three months later, I had somewhat settled into the mundane life that characterizes capitalist modernity in Europe. Once again, I awoke in a startled state, throwing off my blanket and being grabbed by an unnerving feeling that something wasn't quite right. It was a painful gut feeling that someone I knew was in trouble. These feelings have engulphed me on a few other occasions in my life, and unexplainably always unfortunately gelled with a tragic reality.

Several hours later, I was walking through an exhibition at the British Library in London set up to mark the 100th anniversary of the Russian Revolution. Upon exiting, I grabbed my phone to check my messages and then scrolled through Facebook, typical of the majority of young people my age who are socialized to spend an excessive amount of time being unsociable on what is paradoxically called 'social media'. I stopped scrolling when I saw a familiar face looking back at me. I was terrified the moment I realized that the yellow background meant that this man's radiant smile was now eternal, one which was given to the exploited and oppressed people of Rojava and the world. I saw his nom-de-guerre Demhat Goldman affixed to the image after the word 'shehid', and then the name I knew him by: Robert Grodt.

I was shocked, taken aback, furious, saddened, confused and deeply conflicted over the news of this heval's passing on the frontlines of the Great Battle for Raqqa. He had only been in a military formation for a little over 3 months. Admittedly though, the feelings that hit me were somewhat less intense than a few months previous when I discovered that my comrade Destan and those I knew from the YPG Press Office had been killed by an attack by the Turkish military on the Karachok mountain. The last time I had actually seen Robert was on that very mountain, in the same compound which had since been destroyed by fascist bombs at the behest of Sultan Erdogan.

Was the pain of loss now something that was being normalized? Or was it that since I was settling into a rather cushy life in the west again, I needed to keep emotional distance from what was taking place in Rojava? I felt a sense of shame imagining that perhaps it was at least partially the latter. Later that day, I spoke to a German journalist colleague of mine who I had spent some time with in Iraq while in transit to the land of the revolution. We shared stories of those who had passed on in the months since, and he told me bluntly, 'I think you're going to start recognizing a lot more people on shehid posters soon.' After all, the battle for Tabqa was ending and the battle for Raqqa really just beginning. YPJ internationalist Kimmie Taylor, though optimistic about victory in Raqqa, said in a deeply sobering way when speaking to *The Guardian* newspaper, 'Hundreds of us will die in Raqqa.' Such is the reality of the harshness of war.

In the days that followed the news of Demhat's martyrdom, I stared into my phone on many occasions, straight into his eyes that lit up his shehid photo. I wondered if when he took that picture for the YPG, he imagined the possibility that people would be seeing that image in his death. How fleeting life here on earth is for those who commit themselves to this degree.

I recalled my brief encounter with Demhat, who was then still simply Robert, when we were departing Iraq for Syria together. I had already met a few Americans who were travelling to join the YPG, among them a former military man and an anarchist, characteristic of the contradictions of this struggle. Robert was lively and passionate from the moment that he introduced himself to me. He was obviously from the US on account of his accent and his mannerisms. As we shook hands, he told me a bit about his life in California before mentioning that he and his partner now lived in New York. He showed me a bracelet that he had been given by PKK cadres the previous day, saying, 'This means a lot to me. A heval gave this to me.'

Although we didn't get the chance to speak for very long, we did share some humorous stories and anecdotes from our journeys so far, and discussed our plans for Rojava. I told him about the journalist work I was hoping to do and the lessons I was hoping to learn to help rekindle my militant spirit. When speaking about the coming battle for Raqqa, he told me squarely that I should consider joining the YPG, saying, 'We could really use the help.' Robert struck me as being a jokester on the one hand, yet also serious and committed to his ideals. For instance, when comrades pointed out that collaborationist KDP forces were in our vicinity later that evening while crossing the border, he looked at me and whispered, 'Everybody shut the fuck up!' even though nobody else was uttering a word. I chuckled, but tried to keep as silent as I possibly could. It was as if we were two school boys, acting mischievously in the middle of the greatest adventure we had ever been on.

Yet, this was no 'adventure' in the sense that a seriousness of intention and purpose was behind both of our trips, particularly his given the precarious nature of the task he had set himself. Within hours, we were in Rojava, and although Robert and I barely knew each other, there's something that bonds comrades together – indeed that turns you into comrades – when undertaking such a trip together. We said goodbye at Mount Karachok, in the presence of YPG and YPJ comrades who were killed less than 2 months later. We embraced tightly, yet quickly, as a car had come that would take him to the military academy. Little did I know that although we entered Syria together, I would have the luxury of leaving with my backpack on my shoulders, while Robert left a hero, his lifeless body lying in a casket but his spirit forever remaining with the people of the country he gave his life to.

It wasn't until his demise that I realized how much he and I had in common. Yes, we were both leftists and Americans who had found themselves in the unfamiliar terrain of Mesopotamia. Aside from this, however, it turned out that Robert was also involved in the Occupy Wall Street movement in New York back in 2011 that I had also participated in. In fact, it was he who was the father of the so-called 'Occubaby', as he and his partner had met during the protests and later had conceived a child together. I wondered if we had ever actually crossed paths more than half a decade before, without realizing it. Maybe we marched together, chanting slogans and wielding placards while trying to rally people to join the cause of the 99 per cent. Perhaps we fought back against the brutality of the police as our comrades were beaten and bruised. Maybe we even shared a jail cell together after the mass arrest on the Brooklyn Bridge back on 1 October 2011.

Robert, like the majority of YPG internationalist fighters, left a video message behind that was released upon his transition to becoming a shehid. Watching the part of his message that addresses his family is particularly moving. Throughout the rest of the video, he expressed sheer enthusiasm for his contribution to the anti-fascist fight as a member of the People's Protection Unions, speaking of his reasons for joining the struggle and the experience of receiving ideological training at the academy before being sent to the frontlines. Yet, when talking about his family, one can detect a feeling of almost guilt. He says sharply, 'to my daughter…I'm sorry I'm not there'. It drives home the humanness of Demhat's contribution and the magnitude of his sacrifice. Here was a brave young soul who hadn't completely cut himself off from his private life or personal obligations, but he realized that even with a 6-month commitment to the Rojava Revolution, there was a chance he wouldn't be returning home to his family. Although his daughter will not have the opportunity to grow up with Robert in her life, his example is certainly one that she can grow up to be proud of.

Of the internationalists I travelled to Rojava with, one whom I felt a particular fondness for, and whom I grew to know fairly well during our first week in Syria before we parted ways when he decided to leave the civil delegation and join the military academy, was Heval Andok, a Catalan leftist from Barcelona. Andok and I would fall out of contact for about 6 months after we exchanged our final 'Serkeftin' followed by a handshake and a hug, until he popped up one day in my messages on a random afternoon. I was relieved to find out he was safe and sound, and now heading back to Europe after his 6 months of service in the YPG. As it turned out, Andok and Demhat had become extremely close while in the academy together, and travelled to the frontlines in Tabqa as part of the newly formed International People's Revolutionary Guerrilla Forces. Andok even carried Demhat's casket at the funeral service in Rojava after his untimely death, before his body was sent across the border to Iraq and then home to the US. Andok spoke with agony in his messages to me about how much he missed Demhat, but concluded in the most serious manner, 'What I do know is that it's much better to die on the battlefield in Rojava than in our homelands.'

Demhat's death, like his life, was admirable, honourable and noble. We can emulate his spirit whether in New York, Barcelona, London or the frontlines of Syria in the anti-fascist struggle. Yes, there were differences between us despite our shared experiences in North America. He was an anarchist. I've long considered myself a communist. Yet, the brutality of fascism in its concrete conditions forced us into a situation where it was what we shared in common that was amplified. We realized we were comrades, not foes; a lesson a great many of the western left can take from the example of the new world that's being constructed in this Middle Eastern geography.

Chapter 13

Post-ISIS, Will the US Soon Abandon Its Kurdish Allies?

On 17 October, the SDF announced the liberation of Raqqa from the reactionary forces of the Islamic State after the so-called 'Great Battle' in which over 600 of their comrades lost their lives. The freeing of the city from the region's most brutal fascistic group was a great moment of jubilation for the forces of the SDF, both in its Arab militias and the predominately Kurdish forces of the People's Protection Units (YPG) and Women's Protection Units (YPJ).

In particular, the role of the YPJ militants served as a staunch reminder that this was a battle that was as much about liberating women from the bondage of slavery as it was to free the city as a whole from the brutality it had endured since 2014. The images of women clad in military fatigues chanting 'Jin Jiyan Azadi' (Woman, Life, Freedom) after taking the central square in Raqqa, along with their compatriots from the Sinjar Women's Units who had joined the battle to avenge the 2014 massacre of their Yezidi sisters in Shengal, was powerful beyond measure. After all, this is where the fascists of Daesh had not long ago committed public executions and showcased the severed heads of their victims. It was impossible to imagine a more radically different juxtaposition of imagery.

Yet, it wasn't just the socialist, feminist forces of the Kurdish-led movement who claimed Raqqa as their victory. The city had been reduced to rubble by the airstrikes of the US-led coalition, who aided the SDF's onslaught on the Islamic State's self-proclaimed capital from the sky. For the US, it was an opportunity to gloat about their role in fighting 'terrorism', much as they attempted to claim responsibility for saving Kobane in January

2015 when the coordination between the YPG/YPJ and US first began. 'Operation Inherent Resolve' was a major success in their book.

The Basis of the US-SDF Alliance

For many socialists across the world, the alliance between the SDF and the US has caused a great deal of confusion and alienation. I've previously written about the western left's inability to understand the dynamics at play in the Syrian war in my article 'YPG and YPJ: Revolutionists or Pawns of the Empire?' A critique that was as much about my previous lack of understanding as it was about a general problem for self-professed revolutionaries and leftists across the world.

To be sure, the cooperation that has existed between forces who share the Kurdistan Workers' Party (PKK) leader Abdullah Ocalan as their ideological leader and the world's foremost imperialist power is a highly unusual and unique situation. The record of the US abroad has generally been one of supporting and arming the most reactionary forces to engage in its conquest of geo-politically significant parts of the world. A cursory look at US-backed coups, interventions and wars around the world gives us a clear indication that the Pentagon is not in the business of generally siding with genuine liberation movements. Any number of examples show us the true nature of the US war machine, from the 'Forgotten War' on the Korean Peninsula from 1950-3, the brutal attempt to suffocate the Vietnamese liberation struggle a decade later, the support for the fascist coup in Chile in 1973, the arming of the Contra forces in Nicaragua throughout the 1980s and more recently the wars in Iraq and Afghanistan. We know very well what the forces of the US empire are.

That being said, perhaps nobody should be able to comprehend just what the intentions and motivations of the US are better than the Kurdish Freedom Movement itself. After all, it was the US under the aegis of President Bill Clinton and the CIA that played a key role in facilitating the international plot against Ocalan in 1999 that led to his capture in Kenya and imprisonment in Turkey that continues to this day. Even while US weapons have flowed to the forces of the YPG and YPJ and the US has engaged in airstrikes in tandem with them, the US is coordinating intelligence and airstrikes with Turkey against PKK cadres in Turkey and Iraq.

The hypocrisy is staggering. If the US was really invested in its partnership with the Kurdish revolutionary movement, it would de-list the PKK as a terrorist organization, refuse to back Turkey's genocidal ambitions in its Kurdish region, and demand the YPG and YPJ-led forces' political wing, the Democratic Union Party, have a seat at the negotiating table at the Geneva talks that will determine the future of Syria.

Yet, this is ultimately not in their interests. The promotion of a socialist-oriented political model in west Asia ultimately runs contrary to the economic requirements of the monopolies, Wall Street and the decision makers in Washington. The PYD and Kurdish Freedom Movement grouped around the Union of Kurdistan Communities (KCK) realize this. It is why they have continuously referred to the alliance with the US as 'tactical', and as a contradiction that will ultimately be irreconcilable.

In an interview with *ANF English* in early November, KCK Executive Committee member Riza Altun commented on the alliance with the US, pointing out that:

the relationship between the US-led coalition and YPG was seen as legitimate and necessary as the alliance between the US and Soviet Union against Hitler's fascism at the time of the World War II. Both sides needed that kind of relationship like the US and the Soviets needed back then. Thus a tactical relationship was developed with the US against ISIS.

In other words, mutual and overlapping interests led both sides to cooperate with each other, even though their ideological perspectives are considerably different, much in the same way as the USSR and western powers united against the threat of Nazi Germany despite the capitalist and socialist systems being ultimately incompatible.

Altun also points out that the KCK is aware that, true to the nature of the US in all the aforementioned interventions across the globe, Washington also had a role in the spread of the Salafist groups such as al-Nusra and Islamic State in Syria and Iraq. After all, the regime-change fixation of the US as it regards Syria has been well documented for decades. Even if the Syrian Ba'ath government has participated to a degree in the US-backed 'war on terror' and has moved in the direction of neoliberal reforms in the era of Bashar al-Assad, the US establishment has still viewed Syria as an example of independence and economic nationalism. This is as unacceptable to the Pentagon as the nationalist governments of Iraq under Saddam Hussein and Libya under Muammar Gaddafi were. Altun is aware that the US nurtured reactionary forces in this quest, stating that when the battle for Kobane started, support for Salafist groups was not only coming from Turkey, but also that 'other powers, particularly the US and Israel were also supporting these groups'. He says that it was only due to major international pressure that ultimately the US decided to intervene and assist the YPG and YPJ in pushing back Islamic State from reaching the Turkish border in Kobane.

To those who had watched as the Obama administration had almost intervened in Syria in September 2013 to bomb Syrian government positions, only to be bombarded by protests both in the streets and in Congress from those wanting to know if this amounted to support for al-Nusra and Islamic State, the intervention of the US in Syria in a 'war on terror' capacity in late 2014 reeked of hypocrisy.

Unfortunately, much of the left that had supported the Kurdish resistance in Kobane now couldn't bring itself to continue its solidarity with the YPG and YPJ. The resistance was no longer 'pure', but was tainted by an association with the forces of the empire. To the droves of keyboard warriors in the comfort of their western coffee shops, the 'Red Kurds' now changed into proxies for the balkanization of Syria and the region. There was no distinction to be made between the YPG and the reactionary Barzani clan in northern Iraq – they were both part of an imperialist onslaught backed by Zionism, even if the YPG had no intention of fighting the Syrian state forces despite occasional skirmishes with the Syrian Arab Army.

US Fury over Raqqa Victory's Dedication to Ocalan

As the jubilation over the Raqqa victory continued in the days after the declaration of its liberation, the YPG and YPJ announced that this historic accomplishment would be dedicated to their leader Abdullah Ocalan. The media arms of both organizations produced videos in which militants spoke at great length and with passion about how important 'Serok Apo' was to the inspiration to achieve victory not only in Raqqa, but in battles over the previous years across northern Syria. The sight of a huge banner in the city's central square was seen by some Arab nationalists as evidence of 'Kurdish colonialism', despite the fact that Ocalan's writings and the Rojava project have moved away from nationalist discourse in favour of advocating a multi-ethnic society in which cooperation between Kurds, Arabs, Assyrians, Turkmen and other nations is paramount.

The campaign to hold up Ocalan as a symbol of the movement and Raqqa victory for the world to see was strategically significant. It was as much about letting the US know that the convictions of the movement will never be compromised. Days later, US Department of Defence spokesperson Major Adrian Rankine-Galloway told *The Global Post*, 'We condemn the display of PKK leader and founder Abdullah Ocalan during the liberation of Raqqa. The United States continues to support our NATO Ally Turkey in its multi-decade struggle against the PKK and recognizes the loss of life Turkey has suffered in that conflict.'

This again reveals the deep level of tensions involved in the tentative alliance, and the fact that despite Turkey's objections to the US arming of the SDF, the Americans were never interested in making a clean break with the second largest army in NATO. While the US and Turkey remain fundamentally on the same team, the differences between the Pentagon and the Kurdish Freedom Movement are far too significant to make for long-term cooperation.

KCK member Altun expounded on these tensions in his *ANF English* interview, saying:

> The freedom struggle of the Kurds in Rojava is based on freedom and equality on a socialist basis. It is the expression of a political path which was developed basing on the brotherhood and unity of peoples. On the other side, the imperialists are fighting to impose their hegemony over the Middle East…This is not a relationship in which the parties support each other but are in constant conflict.

These hardly sound the words of the leader of a proxy force blindly following the orders of its puppet master and willing to fulfil the needs of its historical mission while rejecting its own.

Altun also referenced once more the example of the western-Soviet cooperation during the Second World War, saying:

> The alliance that was developed during the World War II was an anti-fascist stance which emerged from the intersection of homeland defence of the Soviet Union under intense attacks and the interests of other anti-fascist powers. This agreement remained in force as long as the fascist attacks continued. But

once the fascism was defeated, all parties returned to their own political positions and moved on in accordance with their respective ideological-political path.

However long the cooperation between the Kurdish Freedom Movement and the US does still exist, there's no question that the YPG and YPJ will ever relinquish their ideological convictions. It would be the makings of a spectacular fantasy and a monumental delusion for Washington to think that the basic views of a 40-year liberation movement written in the blood of tens of thousands of martyrs can be undone due to the requests of American imperial arrogance.

Speaking to the Aspen Institute in July, Raymond 'Tony' Thomas, Commander, US Special Operations Command condescendingly told the Kurds fighting in Syria, 'You cannot hold onto Ocalan.' Perhaps WikiLeaks' own Julian Assange said it best when he responded by saying, 'Who is #Ocalan that the US military says the Kurds cannot hold onto? He's their Mandela. US has more chance of giving up George Washington.'

Is the Writing on the Wall?

The Kurds have a saying that their only friends are the mountains. They have been used and marginalized by occupying and colonizing powers for decades, indeed for centuries. The division of their historic homeland into four nation-states almost 100 years ago is only the most recent version of a history of subjugation. It would be wrong to assume that the movement has not understood that at some point after the defeat of Islamic State, this situation of being 'friendless' could again be a very real prospect.

The writing for a shift in US policy towards the SDF – or at least the YPG and YPJ – could already be on the wall. On 13 November, almost a month after the liberation of Raqqa had been declared and long after the Americans had already reacted angrily to its dedication to Ocalan, the BBC published an alleged expose called 'Raqqa's Dirty Secret'. The story itself was far from dirty, far from a secret. Its fundamental premise was that there was an agreement between the SDF and Islamic State to see the evacuation of hundreds of these fascistic militants from the city. This had already been published by dozens of English-language news outlets in the days after it was announced publicly by the SDF. Could the re-packaging of an old story as a ground breaking 'investigation' to make the SDF look 'dirty' have cynical motivations?

YPJ internationalist Kimmie Taylor, who has taken part in multiple campaigns with her Kurdish comrades including the Great Battle for Raqqa, said of the report that it lacked credibility, as it consisted of:

> interviews with drivers and smugglers only concerned with money. In other news, thousands and thousands of YPG and SDF fighters have been alone over the course of 6 years, dying in order to save humanity from ISIS. Funny how now, after we have effectively defeated ISIS, do the media and west begin to turn against us. Think about that for a minute.

No matter what happens next, the Kurdish movement will continue to fight for the same principles of socialism, gender equality, multi-ethnic unity and an ecological society. It held these positions long before the US decided to offer its half-hearted support, and it will continue to hold them long after this military aid has ended. The global left owes it to its own movements to understand the nature of this relationship, and to realize that modern revolutionaries such as Mehmet Aksoy, whose blood is now nourishing the soil in Raqqa, died for a brighter future for all of humanity, not for the interests of imperialism.

Chapter 14

Final Word: A Pledge to Mehmet and to Humanity

I'm convinced that there is at least one place that every aspiring or legitimate revolutionary goes – whether in a physical sense or in the complex web that is their mind – that serves as a source of profound inspiration, of clarity, of militant regeneration when the circumstances of the struggle require it. In our western metropoles, the concrete jungles that represent simultaneously the pinnacle and decadence of capitalist modernity, it is often a daily fight to simply maintain liberatory convictions – not to mention *ethics* – swimming against the tide of rampant individualism and selfishness.

In this sense, I have long felt – as I'm sure so many other young revolutionary minded souls have – that we have largely failed in this struggle; and yet, many of us continue to push forward, attempting to overcome our own aggravating contradictions and become better human beings who are more in line with our political convictions that often run considerably ahead of our practice. There have been more than a few occasions where myself and countless others I know to be the best-intentioned of comrades have considered simply throwing in the towel, accepting the perceived limitations of this society; of discarding revolutionary socialist convictions for the liberalism that often comes to be embodied in a social-democratic framework. The pressures of this society, the drudgery of the daily grind, the allure of the propaganda of the 1 per cent all puts immense pressure on us to 'mature' to a point where we forfeit any thoughts of a full overhaul of capitalism, and find ourselves content with reformism and mere scraps.

I have to admit that the past several years have been

tumultuous in terms of my struggles in this regard. However, I am one of the fortunate ones. I was able to experience a revolution so full, so earth-shattering and so profound that I have been given a new lease on a shot at revolutionary life. This personal and political regeneration came about this spring when I experienced the living, breathing, non-dogmatic and genuine democratic and social process of complete change taking place in northern Syria. In a sense, it was what I had been searching for my entire life.

This isn't to gloss over contradictions, shortcomings, mistakes, or complexities in the process that is the Rojava Revolution, or to throw a materialist understanding of it to the wind in favour of an idealized view that is rosy and romanticized. Yet, I cannot understate how important my 6 weeks in Kurdistan were in terms of reviving my faith not only in revolutionary change, but in the fact that humanity is fundamentally decent and capable of a cooperative and harmonious social order. Witnessing this process did not stop short of reviving my spirit, of nurturing my soul which has been beaten, bruised and battered in the confines of western life.

It's now been more than 7 months since my return to the 'garden society of capitalist modernity', the United Kingdom. There hasn't been a single day that I have risen in which the first thought on my mind hasn't been the struggle of the Kurdish, Arab, Armenian, Assyrian and other nationalities who are carving out the future in the geography of Mesopotamia. In this sense, I certainly left my heart in Qamishlo, Derik, Kobane and the countless other cities of Rojava. I left my spirit somewhere along the Tigris, my soul somewhere in the mountains that Kurds say are their only friends. It also seems that my tears have never left my face in this timeframe – it's difficult to conceive of the fact that so many of the beautiful people I met while finding my own regeneration and sense of purpose have since passed on to another sphere of existence, now to be the faces emblazoned on posters with a yellow or green background. Their contributions are eternal, their status as revolutionaries solidified and ossified in their death.

Monuments That Nurture the Radical Soul

There are two places in the beautiful monstrosity that is the capitalist west where I have felt most connected to the essence of socialist construction during the past decade. These are the physical places where I can travel to that will help to rekindle the flame of militancy within me when it is waning and under threat of being blown out.

The first of these is the Soviet war memorial in Treptower Park, Berlin, home to 7,000 young men and women who perished in the battle to liberate the city from the grip of Hitlerlite fascism. Setting foot in this memorial makes one think of the fleeting nature of life, the sacrifice of an entire generation of Soviet youth to not only defend socialism in the USSR, but the democratic aspirations of people across Europe of various political stripes. The impressiveness of this memorial is awe-inspiring, a testament to a belief that after such darkness and tragedy, the building of a new, better world is indeed possible.

The second place in which I have felt the power of a rekindling of my progressive fervour is at the grave of Karl Marx at Highgate Cemetery in north London. Marx's contributions to the understanding of how the oppressed can break free from the shackles of exploitation more than 150 years ago continue to agitate, annoy and create panic in the dark hearts of the brutal despots of this world. As I live in London at this point in my life, Marx's grave has been a place I have visited frequently. The serene scenery allows for quiet contemplation, self-critique and reflection. It is a point of spiritual pilgrimage to which I have brought comrades from across Europe and North America. Not only is it home to Marx, but of other revolutionaries who followed in his footsteps, from Claudia Jones to cadres of the South African Communist Party who fought against the brutality of the apartheid system that they helped to relegate to the dustbin of history.

Mehmet Joins Marx

As of 10 November 2017, Highgate Cemetery has taken on a much more deeply personal connection and relevance than it ever did before. On that brisk yet sunny, contradictory Friday, I entered the cemetery for perhaps the tenth or eleventh time in the span of the last 4 years. However, unlike my previous trips in which I either came on my own or was accompanied by one or two other people, on this occasion I was in a sea of thousands. In this sea, it didn't seem as if we were collectively travelling against the tide, but with it for once. It was a sea of solemn vibrancy, of green, of yellow, of red – especially red. It was the culmination of a transcontinental journey for a twenty-first century revolutionary who was preparing to be laid to rest. This man was my friend, my comrade, my brother, a source of profound inspiration and support. Heval Mehmet Aksoy. Sometimes known as Firaz Dag. Always known as genuine, as selfless, as the epitome of all that we can aspire to be ourselves.

Yes, I've cried for Mehmet, on more than just one occasion. The news of his death on 26 September provoked feelings of shock, of outrage, of a desire for revenge against the fascists who took his life as they have taken the lives of so many of our comrades. It provoked great personal sadness, feelings of confusion, even perhaps selfishly feelings that the book he was helping me write and edit wouldn't be completed in the way that it would have had he not been taken from us. These feelings, however, particularly those of confusion, began to ebb the moment his body was lowered into the ground. To see the faces of his family so distraught is to see the faces of the countless mothers, fathers, sons, daughters, brothers and sisters of the martyrs of Kurdistan, the martyrs of Palestine, of Latin America, Africa, of Asia. It is to witness the effects that the struggle has had on the collective consciousness and soul of the downtrodden of this planet.

I left Highgate that day as flowers were still being thrown onto his grave, as his body was just beginning to settle into its permanent home. I returned the next day to try to find a sense of closure. The process I was experiencing, though, was simultaneously one of finally coming to grips with a personal loss, as well as developing myself politically, and hopefully ethically. There's nothing wrong with tears being shed for our comrades. In and of themselves, however, they frankly mean nothing. They certainly don't contribute to enhancing, developing or taking up Mehmet's legacy, which is one which is intertwined with and inextricably linked to the legacy of each human being who has fallen in the fight for a more just world order.

The Collision of Highgate with Rojava

Rojava and Highgate Cemetery, Mehmet and Marx, now collide and intersect in the reality of life and in my deepest being. At the memorial service at the Kurdish Community Centre just hours before he was buried, countless speakers alluded to the collective necessity of continuing the work that Heval Memo left behind. It was said at one juncture that we ought to be ashamed of ourselves every time we choose comfort over the difficulty of struggle. This echoes the words of Mehmet himself when he said:

> I want to be in Kurdistan in the next few years. Whatever I do, I want it to be there. If we don't get what our people sacrificed for in the next few years, I'm afraid that I will live in shame for the rest of my life. We have a role to play, and that's all we need to do. Easy? No, but well worth it.

He understood very well that unless he dedicated himself fully to the liberation of his people, ultimately his words would have been hollow. I, too, understand on a basic level that any number of words alone that I write, that help to express at least somewhat the sentiments and convictions in my heart, mean very little in the final analysis unless they are combined with struggle; unless they are combined with concrete contributions to the most advanced freedom struggle our world knows at this stage. If my experiences in Rojava helped to bring me a much more thoroughgoing rekindling of revolutionary convictions than the temporary sparks given to me by the Soviet war memorial or Marx's grave could have, the reality of Highgate with its newest resident – the best son of Rojava and Kurdistan – has shaken me to such an extent that I feel the need to pledge myself much more thoroughly to the freedom struggle that he dedicated, and in the end, sacrificed his life to.

Mehmet's Ethics, Convictions and Practice

I often re-visit the messages between Mehmet and myself in order to not only remember him but to read deeper into what motivated him and the way he related to people. Most of these had to do with the book project we were hoping to complete by the end of 2017. This undoubtedly is a book that now needs to manifest, even though just prior to his death I began having second thoughts about whether my writing such a volume about Rojava was presumptuous considering that as it stands now, I have only spent what is ultimately a very short period of time there. Yet, Memo was always supportive and encouraging, asking that I put aside any objections I might feel to my own lack of confidence.

Ironically, however, I'm not sure that he actually knew how valuable his own contributions were when he travelled to Rojava and put himself in the crossfire in order to tell the stories that humanity was writing in blood. His final message to me, exactly 1 week before his martyrdom, is worth repeating again: 'Heval Marcel, thank you for your warming message and kindness. I hope I am being of some good.'

This was deeply characteristic of him. I'm sure that being in the land of revolution had only nurtured his humility, humble spirit and collective nature – in some ways, one can never move fully into that domain until one is cut off from the individualism of our reactionary society. Still, Mehmet seemed to have exhibited these very rare characteristics even while growing up and coming of age in the jungle and labyrinth of darkness that is London. How he grew to such a stature in this world is beyond me, but it does explain the great sense of sadness he held onto while in the west, the feelings of being incomplete, and why he felt he needed to not only do more, but travel to where he knew his spirit would be set on fire.

Mehmet said in his final weeks of life, 'In the midst of death, I am very close to life.' It is true that not everyone who wants to contribute to the Kurdish Freedom Movement or to the larger struggle for a socialist world needs to play the frontline role that Memo was willing to. This would frankly be unrealistic. We often think of revolution from the relative comfort of our western cafes and homes in an ultra-leftist, even romanticized sense as simply grabbing the gun. To be sure, the gun is indispensable in the fight across Kurdistan, and nobody should fear the legitimate right of self-defence. However, as Rojava taught me, sometimes the most revolutionary act someone can contribute is cooking breakfast for the collective, cleaning the toilets when it isn't your turn to do so out of selfless initiative, striking up a conversation with a heval whom you may not often see eye to eye with, listening when you're accustomed to spending too much time speaking. In this sense, everyone can learn from Rojava, but also from Memo.

Before he wore the uniform of the YPG and carried both a Kalashnikov and a camera, he spoke in front of crowds at protests and forums, becoming a household name in the Kurdish movement in Europe. He also worked behind his laptop on projects in which sometimes he was named, other times where his contribution was anonymous. Throughout it all, he was profoundly human – not robotic, rigid, dogmatic or black and white. He was a walking contradiction like all of us, but one who was always striving to resolve the most profound of these.

Continuing Heval Mehmet's Work

The fundamental defect of the fascist mentality is that these regressive forces believe that the killing of individual resisters brings them a step closer to consolidating the disgusting, anti-human world they aspire to create. They have historically been mistaken, and to their inevitable frustration they will continue to be.

It will be difficult, perhaps even impossible, to fill Mehmet's shoes as an individual – however, as was evident by the thousands who attended his funeral, there are scores who are willing to collectively contribute to upholding and advancing the project he fought for. It should be pointed out that about a century and a half after his death, and even despite the overthrow of so-called actually existing socialism more than 25 years ago, Marx's grave continues to be almost a religious-like point of pilgrimage for communists and socialists the world over. Mehmet deserves to be in the company of Marx and those who came after him; outside of the geography of Kurdistan, it is difficult to imagine a more suitable place of rest for his body. Both of their graves will now be a place the oppressed of the world can visit to make a pledge to dedicate themselves more fully to the achievement of the kind of world we truly deserve to live in.

Mehmet's death should be a call to action, a battle cry to pick up his gun, his camera, his pen. It should be a call to not allow the beauty of his smile to ever vanish from this earth. It should serve as the most profound inspiration to all aspiring revolutionaries to be revolutionaries in *deed*. All who were touched by his existence and his example should deepen our commitment to the liberation of the wretched of the earth. This is our historic duty and obligation in the face of the fascists whom we shall deal a deathblow. In the immortal words of Bobby Sands, 'Our revenge shall be the laughter of our children.'

Shehid Namirin!

Mehmet Aksoy is Eternal

Zero Books

CULTURE, SOCIETY & POLITICS

Contemporary culture has eliminated the concept and public figure of the intellectual. A cretinous anti-intellectualism presides, cheer-led by hacks in the pay of multinational corporations who reassure their bored readers that there is no need to rouse themselves from their stupor. Zer0 Books knows that another kind of discourse – intellectual without being academic, popular without being populist – is not only possible: it is already flourishing. Zer0 is convinced that in the unthinking, blandly consensual culture in which we live, critical and engaged theoretical reflection is more important than ever before.

If you have enjoyed this book, why not tell other readers by posting a review on your preferred book site.

Recent bestsellers from Zero Books are:

In the Dust of This Planet
Horror of Philosophy vol. 1
Eugene Thacker
In the first of a series of three books on the Horror of
Philosophy, *In the Dust of This Planet* offers the genre of horror
as a way of thinking about the unthinkable.
Paperback: 978-1-84694-676-9 ebook: 978-1-78099-010-1

Capitalist Realism
Is there no alternative?
Mark Fisher
An analysis of the ways in which capitalism has presented itself
as the only realistic political-economic system.
Paperback: 978-1-84694-317-1 ebook: 978-1-78099-734-6

Rebel Rebel
Chris O'Leary
David Bowie: every single song. Everything you want to know,
everything you didn't know.
Paperback: 978-1-78099-244-0 ebook: 978-1-78099-713-1

Cartographies of the Absolute
Alberto Toscano, Jeff Kinkle
An aesthetics of the economy for the twenty-first century.
Paperback: 978-1-78099-275-4 ebook: 978-1-78279-973-3

Malign Velocities
Accelerationism and Capitalism
Benjamin Noys
Long listed for the Bread and Roses Prize 2015, *Malign Velocities* argues against the need for speed, tracking acceleration as the symptom of the ongoing crises of capitalism.
Paperback: 978-1-78279-300-7 ebook: 978-1-78279-299-4

Meat Market
Female Flesh under Capitalism
Laurie Penny
A feminist dissection of women's bodies as the fleshy fulcrum of capitalist cannibalism, whereby women are both consumers and consumed.
Paperback: 978-1-84694-521-2 ebook: 978-1-84694-782-7

Poor but Sexy
Culture Clashes in Europe East and West
Agata Pyzik
How the East stayed East and the West stayed West.
Paperback: 978-1-78099-394-2 ebook: 978-1-78099-395-9

Sweetening the Pill
or How we Got Hooked on Hormonal Birth Control
Holly Grigg-Spall
Has contraception liberated or oppressed women? *Sweetening the Pill* breaks the silence on the dark side of hormonal contraception.
Paperback: 978-1-78099-607-3 ebook: 978-1-78099-608-0

Why Are We The Good Guys?
Reclaiming your Mind from the Delusions of Propaganda
David Cromwell
A provocative challenge to the standard ideology that Western
power is a benevolent force in the world.
Paperback: 978-1-78099-365-2 ebook: 978-1-78099-366-9

Readers of ebooks can buy or view any of these bestsellers by
clicking on the live link in the title. Most titles are published
in paperback and as an ebook. Paperbacks are available in
traditional bookshops. Both print and ebook formats are
available online.

Find more titles and sign up to our readers' newsletter
at http://www.johnhuntpublishing.com/culture-and-politics

Follow us on Facebook
at https://www.facebook.com/ZeroBooks

and Twitter at https://twitter.com/Zer0Books